P9-DUZ-434

The Scarecrow Author Bibliographies

JOHN BARTH:
An Annotated Bibliography

by

RICHARD ALLAN VINE

Scarecrow Author Bibliographies, No. 31

The Scarecrow Press, Inc.

Metuchen, N.J.   1977

Library of Congress Cataloging in Publication Data

Vine, Richard Allan, 1948-
    John Barth: an annotated bibliography.

    (Scarecrow author bibliographies ; no. 31)
    Includes index.
    1.   Barth, John--Bibliography.
Z8076. 7. V55 [PS3552. A75]   016. 813'5'4   76-55322
ISBN 0-8108-1003-4

CONTENTS

INTRODUCTION

Twenty years have now elapsed since the release of John Barth's first published novel, The Floating Opera. The book, which had been rejected by numerous editors and finally accepted by Appleton-Century-Crofts only upon the stipulation that its ending be softened, was considered by reviewers to be at once impressive (though not necessarily successful), bizarre, and morally suspect. With due allowance for increasing critical momentum, that same pattern of mixed and often impassioned reaction has greeted each of Barth's five subsequent productions. John Barth is not an author who inspires indifference. To some he is a genius (perhaps a pernicious one), to some a pedant, and to some a fraud. The currently widening acceptance of his work is indicative of a generally accelerating receptiveness to non-realistic fiction-- a receptiveness which that work has to a large degree helped to foster.

In the period immediately following the publication of The Floating Opera and The End of the Road, Barth was something of a literary cult figure, evoking the admiration of an enthusiastic but relatively minute readership. Then, rather suddenly in 1960, the unlikely success of The Sot-Weed Factor--still his most uniformly esteemed work--thrust Barth into the very center of serious critical attention, a position he has continued to occupy for all informed observers of post-World War II American fiction. A 1963 special issue of Critique (volume 6, number 2) confirmed Barth's new status as a major contemporary figure by bringing together the first group of scholarly articles on his work. Three years later, Giles Goat-Boy (1966) became Barth's first immediate commercial success, selling 50,000 copies in the original hardbound edition, garnering exceptionally wide reviews, and justifying paperback promotion as a best seller.

The year following the publication of Giles Goat-Boy may legitimately be regarded as the occasion of Barth's liter-

ary confirmation, for in 1967 his first three novels were re-
issued in revised editions, including, most significantly, a
restoration of the originally intended ending of The Floating
Opera. Concurrently, Robert Scholes published his widely
read study, The Fabulators, which contains an extensive
apology for Barth's peculiar artistic strategy. Since that
time, Barth's extension of his early formalist tendencies into
the multimedia experiments of Lost in the Funhouse (1968)
and the extreme narrative complexities of Chimera (1972) have
made him a virtual cultural institution of the post-modernist
period--the most abundantly gifted representative of an aesthetic with which anyone writing (or writing about) literature
today must contend. Reviews, articles, book chapters, commentary in surveys, and dissertations have of course pro-
liferated, and at least one full volume devoted entirely to
Barth has already appeared (see D14). Finally, if viewed
optimistically, the selection of Chimera as a National Book
Award winner may be taken as prefiguring Barth's eventual
establishment as a standard American author.

About the Bibliography

        This bibliography is designed, very consciously, as a
tool to aid researchers whose ends are interpretive rather
than inventorial. Its emphasis, therefore, is upon those
items--book reviews and articles--at once most essential and
most elusive for the investigative scholar. Ideally, the
book's arrangement offers both a ready profile of critical response and a collection of fairly specific individual synopses.
From such a dualistic source, most researchers should be
able to determine which entries are germane to their own
critical projects.

        Since there is at present no other annotated Barth bib-
liography available, I have attempted to make this one as full
as possible. I make no claim, however, to exhaustiveness--
first, because only a professional bibliographer could confi-
dently have kept track of all the material relevant to this
burgeoning field of interest; second, because I have deliberately kept my focus tight. I have included only those items
devoted exclusively or at least substantially to John Barth.
Only occasionally, when the commentary seemed particularly
significant, have I included more comprehensive studies that
make general or passing reference to Barth. My annotations
of books tend more to be descriptive than synoptic because
books are, in most cases, comparatively easy for the re-

searcher to locate and comparatively difficult for the bibliographer to summarize. Readers interested in the section on doctoral dissertations should be aware that it encompasses only those theses entered in Dissertation Abstracts International, a listing to which not all universities contribute.

Special acknowledgment must be given to two previous Barth bibliographies. Jackson R. Bryer's "Two Bibliographies" in Critique, vol. 6, no. 2 (fall 1963) was especially helpful in locating obscure book reviews of Barth's first three novels. John N. Weixlmann's "John Barth: A Bibliography" in Critique, vol. 13, no. 3 (summer 1972) is the most comprehensive work of its sort currently available, including many references only tangentially related to Barth. His work is, quite literally, the basis of my own.

The expression of my own evaluations of John Barth's work I leave to a future date. For now it is enough, I hope, to have supplied to other students of post-modernism this preliminary report on one section of the critical landscape before us.

Richard Allan Vine
University of Chicago
March 1976

PRIMARY SOURCES

BOOKS

<u>The Floating Opera</u>

A1.   New York: Appleton-Century-Crofts, 1956.

A2.   Toronto: S. J. R. Saunders, 1956.

A3.   New York: Avon Books, 1956 (pa.).

Revised Edition:

A4.   Garden City, N. Y. : Doubleday & Co. , 1967.

A5.   Toronto: Doubleday, Canada, 1967.

A6.   London: Martin, Secker & Warburg, 1968.

A7.   New York: Avon Books, 1969 (pa.).

A8.   Harmondsworth, Middlesex: Penguin Books, 1970 (pa.).

A9.   New York: Bantam Books, 1972 (pa.).

<u>The End of the Road</u>

A10.   Garden City, N. Y. : Doubleday & Co. , 1958.

A11.   Toronto: Doubleday, Canada, 1958.

A12.   New York: Avon Books, 1960 (pa.).

A13.   London: Secker & Warburg, 1962.

A14.   London: Brown & Watson, 1964 (pa.).

A15.   New York: Avon Books, 1964 (pa.).

Revised Edition:

A16.   Garden City, N. Y. : Doubleday & Co. , 1967.

1

A17.   Harmondsworth, Middlesex: Penguin Books, 1967 (pa.).

A18.   Toronto: Doubleday, Canada, 1967.

A19.   New York: Bantam Books, 1969 (pa.).

A20.   New York: Grosset & Dunlap, 1969 (pa.).

The Sot-Weed Factor

A21.   Garden City, N. Y. : Doubleday & Co. , 1960.

A22.   Toronto: Doubleday, Canada, 1960.

A23.   London: Secker & Warburg, 1961.

A24.   New York: Grosset & Dunlap, 1964 (pa.).

A25.   Toronto: George J. McLeod, 1964 (pa.).

A26.   London: Panther Books, 1965 (pa.).

A27.   New York: Grosset & Dunlap, 1966 (pa.).

Revised Edition:

A28.   Garden City, N. Y. : Doubleday & Co. , 1967.

A29.   Toronto: Doubleday, Canada, 1967.

A30.   New York: Bantam Books, 1969 (pa.).

Giles Goat-Boy; or, The Revised New Syllabus

A31.   Garden City, N. Y. : Doubleday & Co. , 1966.

A32.   Garden City, N. Y. : Doubleday & Co. , 1966 (limited
       edition: numbered, signed).

A33.   Greenwich, Conn. : Fawcett, 1967 (pa.).

A34.   London: Secker & Warburg, 1967.

A35.   Harmondsworth, Middlesex: Penguin Books, 1968 (pa.).

A36.   Greenwich, Conn. : Fawcett, 1971 (pa.).

A37.   Greenwich, Conn. : Fawcett, 1974 (pa.).

Lost in the Funhouse:
Fiction for Print, Tape, Live Voice

A38.   Garden City, N. Y. : Doubleday & Co. , 1968.

A39.   Garden City, N.Y.: Doubleday & Co., 1968 (limited
          edition: numbered, signed).

A40.   Toronto: Doubleday, Canada, 1968.

A41.   London: Secker & Warburg, 1969.

A42.   New York: Bantam Books, 1969 (pa.).

A43.   New York: Grosset & Dunlap, 1969 (pa.).

Chimera

A44.   New York: Random House, 1972 (limited edition).

A45.   New York: Fawcett, 1972 (pa.).

SHORT FICTION

A46.   "Lilith and the Lion," The Hopkins Review, 4 (fall
          1950), 49-53.

A47.   "The Remobilization of Jacob Horner," Esquire, 50
          (July 1958), 55-59.

A48.   "Landscape: The Eastern Shore," The Kenyon Review,
          22 (1960), 104-10.

A49.   "Ambrose His Mark," Esquire, 59 (February 1963),
          122-27.

A50.   "Water-Message," Southwest Review, 48 (1963), 226-
          37.

A51.   "Night-Sea Journey," Esquire, 65 (June 1966), 82-83,
          147-48.

A52.   "Test Borings," Modern Occasions, ed. Philip Rahv
          (New York: Farrar, Straus, & Giroux, 1966), pp.
          247-63.

A53.   "Lost in the Funhouse," The Atlantic Monthly, 220
          (November 1967), 73-82. Reprinted in Rust Hills,
          ed. Writer's Choice (New York: David McKay,
          1974), pp. 3-24.

A54.   "Autobiography: A Self-Recorded Fiction," New Amer-
          ican Review, no. 2 (1968), 72-75.

A55.   "Petition," Esquire, 70 (July 1968), 68-71, 135.

A56.   "Title," The Yale Review, 57 (winter 1968), 213-21.

A57.   "Help! A Stereophonic Narrative for Authorial Voice,"
       Esquire, 72 (September 1969), 108-09.

A58.   "Dunyazadiad," Esquire, 77, 463 (June 1972), 136-42,
       158-68.

A59.   "Perseid," Harper's Magazine, 245, 1469 (October
       1972), 79-96.

A60.   "Bellerophoniad" (excerpt), Fiction, 1, 2 (1972).

A61.   "Life-Story," Reprinted in Philip Stevick, ed. Anti-
       Story: An Anthology of Experimental Fiction (New
       York: Free Press, 1971), pp. 3-15, and in Joe
       David Bellamy, ed. Superfiction, or The American
       Story Transformed: An Anthology (New York: Ran-
       dom, 1975), pp. 197-212.

NONFICTION

A62.   "My Two Muses," Johns Hopkins Magazine, 12 (April
       1961), 9-13.

A63.   "Afterword," The Adventures of Roderick Random by
       Tobias Smollett (New York: New American Library-
       Signet Classics, 1964), pp. 469-79.

A64.   "Muse Spare Me," Book Week, September 26, 1965,
       pp. 28-29.

A65.   "A Gift of Books," Holiday, 40 (December 1966), 171-
       72, 174, 177 [especially 171].

A66.   "Censorship--1967: A Series of Symposia," Arts in
       Society, 4 (1967), 265-358 [especially 294].

A67.   "The Literature of Exhaustion," Atlantic Monthly, 220
       (August 1967), 29-34. Reprinted in Marcus Klein,
       ed. The American Novel Since World War II (New
       York: Fawcett Publication, 1969), pp. 267-79, and
       in Raymond Federman, ed. Surfiction: Fiction Now
       ... and Tomorrow (Chicago: Swallow Press, 1975),
       pp. 19-33.

A68.   A Tribute to Vladimir Nabokov. In Nabokov: Criti-
       cism, Reminiscences, Translations and Tributes,
       Alfred Appel, Jr. and Charles Newman, eds.

(Evanston, Ill.: Northwestern University Press, 1970), p. 350.

A69. "A Tribute to John Hawkes," Harvard Advocate, 104 (October 1970), 11.

A70. Preface to "Lost in the Funhouse," in Rust Hills, ed. Writer's Choice (New York: David McKay, 1974), pp. 1-2.

INTERVIEWS AND STATEMENTS

A71. Golwyn, Judith. "New Creative Writers: 35 Novelists Whose First Work Appears This Season," Library Journal, 81, 11 (June 1, 1956), 1496-97.

A72. Enck, John J. "John Barth: An Interview," Wisconsin Studies in Contemporary Literature, 6 (1965), 3-14.

A73. Meras, Phyllis. "John Barth: A Truffle No Longer," New York Times Book Review, August 7, 1966, p. 22.

A74. "Heroic Comedy," Newsweek, August 8, 1966, pp. 81-82. [especially 82].

A75. Price, Alan. "An Interview with John Barth," Prism (George Washington University), spring 1968, 50-51.

A76. "L'Ombre di Sheherazade: Conversazione con John Barth," La Fiera Letteraria, July 18, 1968, pp. 2-3.

A77. Davis, Douglas M. "The End Is a Beginning for Barth's 'Funhouse,' " National Observer, September 16, 1968, p. 19.

A78. Henkle, Roger. "Symposium Highlights: Wrestling (American Style) with Proteus," Novel, 3, 3 (1970), 197-207 [especially 199, 205].

A79. Bellamy, Joe David. "Algebra and Fire: An Interview with John Barth," The Falcon, 4 (Spring 1972).

A80. _____. "Having It Both Ways: A Conversation Between John Barth and Joe David Bellamy," New
American Review, no. 15 (1972), 134-50.

A81. _____. "John Barth," The New Fiction: Interviews with Innovative American Writers (Urbana:
University of Illinois Press, 1974), pp. 1-18. Re-
print of A80.

A82. Shenker, Israel. "Complicated Simple Things," New
York Times Book Review, September 24, 1972, pp.
35-38.

A83. "John Barth," First Person: Conversations on Writers
and Writing, Frank Gado, ed. (Schenectady, N.Y.:
Union College Press, 1973), pp. 110-41.

PAPERS

A84. "John Barth Papers," Quarterly Journal of the Library
of Congress, 26 (1969), 247-49.

RECORDINGS

A85. John Barth Reads from Giles Goat-Boy (New York:
CMS Records, 1968), LP Disc: #551.

A86. Prose Readings by John Barth (New York: McGraw-
Hill, 1970), tape: cassette #81575, reel to reel
#75988.

A87. Two Narratives for Tape and Live Voice (New York:
McGraw-Hill, 1970), tape: cassette #81673, reel
to reel #78162.

A88. Novelist John Barth: Mythology Recycled for Today,
(North Hollywood, Calif.: Audio-Text Cassettes,
1975), cassette #31810.

SECONDARY SOURCES

BOOK REVIEWS

THE FLOATING OPERA

B1   Adelman, George.   "Barth, John.   The Floating Opera,"
     under "Fiction," Library Journal, 81, 14 (1956),
     1789.

     "There is something of Céline in the picaresque
events and of Camus in the 'absurdist' philosophy of the book,
and even something of Sterne in the humor.   But it is not
all successful.   The author seems too self-consciously trying to shock, and his casual, friendly style is sometimes in-
congruous. "

B2   Bradbury, Malcolm.   "The Human Comedy," Guardian
     Weekly, 99, 15 (October 10, 1968), 14.

     Although Todd Andrews is "one of those philosophical
men of no feeling that come up elsewhere in Barth," the book
also pays homage to the "joyous enjoyment" of seaboard life.

B3   "Comic Opera," Omaha World-Herald, January 13,
     1957, p. G29.

B4   Cooper, Madison.   "Chockfull of Curiosities," Dallas
     Morning News, October 14, 1956, part 5, p. 15.

B5   "First Novel Inspired by Famous Showboat," Springfield
     Sunday Republican, August 12, 1956, p. C12.

B6   "The Floating Opera," Kirkus, 24, 12 (June 15, 1956),
     417.

     "A deliberately digressive and, on occasion, smugly
salacious report on the life and times of Todd Andrews, a

7

bachelor, a lawyer, and a philosopher of (and out of) sorts who reviews his life as it was influenced by a heart condition and prostate trouble. "

B7   "The Floating Opera," under "Paperbacks," Observer Review, February 15, 1970, p. 26.

        The reissuance of this novel gives the reader the opportunity to "talent-spot with hindsight. "

B8   "The Floating Opera: Revised Edition," Publishers Weekly, 191, 10 (March 6, 1967), 73.

        In this edition Barth "has restored the original ending and made a number of what seem to this reader to be relatively minor changes. " The book "remains an interesting first novel by an author of promise. " Giles Goat-Boy (which, along with The Sot-Weed Factor, may consider the fulfillment of that promise) is "a rather surprising omission from this year's list of fiction contenders for National Book Award honors. "

B9   Freedley, George. Morning Telegraph (New York), August 28, 1956, p. 2.

B10   Graham, Kenneth. "Frayn's a Caution, " The Listener, 80, 2062 (October 3, 1968), 449.

        Barth's 1956 novel, now published in Britain for the first time, manifests an "expertise and aplomb" truly remarkable in a beginning writer. "But the matrix of the book remains an intellectual attitude, not a felt urge to create a living world. "

B11   Harding, Walter. "Needless Vulgarity in Novel," Chicago Sunday Tribune Magazine of Books, October 21, 1956, part 4, p. 14.

        "If prizes were offered for strangely constructed novels, this one would win hands down. ... I doubt if anyone will question Barth's cleverness. He shows more ability in handling the structure of his novel than I have seen in a long time. " Lack of confidence, unfortunately, has led Barth to "stoop to sensationalism and vulgarity" which add nothing to the characters or structure of the novel.

B12   Hogan, William. "A Bookman's Notebook--Life Is a

Showboat, a Young Author Finds," <u>San Francisco Chronicle</u>, August 28, 1956, p. 19.

B13 Hyman, Stanley Edgar. "John Barth's First Novel," <u>New Leader</u>, April 12, 1965, pp. 20-21.

The Floating Opera is pervaded by a variation of "the Albertine Strategy," that is, "an affair with a man variously disguised as an affair with a woman." In this case, as in Joyce, "two male friends attain symbolic union by sharing the body of a woman." Later "the covert, symbolic homosexuality of The Floating Opera ... becomes the mad polymorphous pansexuality of The Sot-Weed Factor." An extensive summary of Barth's first novel confirms that it is "quite an achievement for a man of 26." Barth's subsequent work suggests that there is scarcely a conceivable limit to his potential.

B14 "Liebestodd," <u>Times Literary Supplement</u>, October 10, 1968, p. 1161.

The Floating Opera is "a virtuoso exercise by a master-puppeteer." Like Joyce, Barth has his action cover a single day, "Todd-day ... Tod-day, death-day." The construction is fugal. Todd's war scene with the German sergeant is "both a spoof and a critique of Melville's Ishmael and Queequeg sharing a bed at the Spouter-Inn." Barth makes a satiric response to the Sisyphe of Camus. "Everything in this existential comedy is 'absurd'.... Everything suggests its contrary. No direction is a final direction." He manages successfully "to reanimate Sterne's dodge of <u>non sequiturs</u> and digressions."

B15 <u>Los Angeles Mirror and Daily News</u>, August 20, 1956, part II, p. 2.

B16 Mandel, Siegfried. "Gaudy Showboat," <u>New York Times Book Review</u>, August 26, 1956, p. 27.

The Floating Opera is a satire with a moral, namely that "it is best to choose among the relative values that life offers rather than cynically rejecting all values by way of suicide." The book is "amusing and revolting in turn," and Mr. Barth has "neatly adapted the techniques and elaborate storytelling paraphernalia of such English eighteenth-century writers as Fielding and Sterne, putting new life into an old genre."

B17 Myers, Art. "Life's But a Showboat Drifting By,"
       Washington Post and Times Herald, August 26, 1956,
       p. E6.

       Todd Andrews is "a character to end all characters."
Except for its "rather turgid" ending in which Todd begins to
take his musing too seriously, "the book is a delightful tour
de force by a new author who, if this is a true measure of
his talent, is going to become well known."

B18 Petersen, Clarence. "The Floating Opera by John
       Barth," under "Pick of the Paperbacks," Washington
       Post Book World, August 6, 1972, p. 13.

       The "uncensored" version of Barth's 1956 novel
"holds many surprises."

B19 Prescott, Orville. "Books of the Times," New York
       Times, September 3, 1956, p. 11.

       "Most of this odd novel is dull. Most of its humor
is labored and flat. Some of its heavy-handed attempts to
shock seem cheap in a juvenile and nasty way rather than
sophisticated or realistic, as they probably were intended."
Much of the book's weakness stems from its seemingly having
been written as an uneasy collaboration between two authors,
one writing "a crude farce heightened by wit," the other a
solemn meditation upon "the meaning of existence."

B20 Price, R. G. G. "New Novels," Punch, 255, 6682
       (October 2, 1968), 487.

       Considered along with three other novels, The Float-
ing Opera is found to be "rather self-indulgently wayward,
though less tangy with fantasy and learning than The Sot-
Weed Factor." Once the "shandean pretensions" are adjusted
to, the book offers some enjoyment. "It is juvenilia but
quite fun on the surface."

B21 Rubin, Louis D., Jr. "Novels of the Eastern Shore
       and War," Baltimore Evening Sun, August 27, 1956,
       p. 16.

B22 Schickel, Richard. "An 'Opera' Afloat," Milwaukee
       Journal, December 30, 1956, part 5, p. 4.

B23 Wall, Stephen. "New Novels," under "The Horrors of

Holovision," Observer Review, September 29, 1968, p. 26.

The revised edition of The Floating Opera is reviewed along with three other novels. Although it is "a mere foothill on the way to the mountainous bulk of 'The Sot-Weed Factor' and 'Giles Goat-Boy,' " the work will nevertheless reward "the scavengers of the seminar" because, despite its humor, "there is something heartless in the very subtlety of its organisation" that seems to demand serious exegesis.

THE END OF THE ROAD

B24   Boatwright, Taliaferro. "Jacob Horner Came Out of His Corner, and Then--," New York Herald Tribune Book Review, July 20, 1958, p. 3.

Barth's book is "at once imaginative, unconventional, penetrating and entertaining." In order to explore the problem of choice in a world devoid of standards, the author has created a plot with developments which are "often hilariously (but mordantly) amusing, occasionally brilliantly illuminating, ultimately almost physically jolting."

B25   Bradbury, Malcolm. "New Novels," Punch, 243, 6370 (October 10, 1962), 540.

The End of the Road is "a very amusing and very profound book, just a little too imitative and unsure to be really important, but of high quality."

B26   Coleman, John. The Queen (London), 221 (September 18, 1962), 27-28.

B27   "The End of the Road," Kirkus, 26, 10 (May 15, 1958), 362.

"Sick-sick-sick, or maybe just foul.... The same road that has been travelled with Kerouac, and to an extent Herbert Gold, this is for those schooled in the waste matter of the body and the mind; for others, a real recoil."

B28   "Fiction by Tyndareus," under "John O'London's Pullout Guide to New Books," John O'London's, 7 (September 27, 1962), p. IV.

B29 Kerner, David. "Psychodrama in Eden," Chicago Review, 13, 1 (1959), 59-67.

The End of the Road is not, strictly speaking, a novel of manners or a novel of ideas, but an "ideological farce," in which an existentialist (Joe Morgan) faces a nihilist (Jake Horner) in a confrontation with distinct overtones of medieval allegory. The book is tremendously engaging and contains many brilliant set-pieces, but cannot finally accomplish its ends because Barth "has made his characters both insane and two-dimensional," whereas, to truly expose an ideology, "the novelist must show its effect on relatively whole human beings, just as a biochemist traces the effects of a virus through the biological systems of a normal organism."

B30 LaHaye, Judson. "Barth, John: The End of the Road," Best Sellers, 18 (August 1, 1958), 165.

Despite its technical excellences, this novel "achieves only a quality of despair." Both setting and characters are "one-dimensional in their surface depths." The prose, although strong, reflects the anguish of situations without sympathetic results" and might well be classified as "beat, lost, and possibly retrogressive." The reader is left without a solution. "This novel is not ordinary in its talent, but neither is it moral or human."

B31 Raven, Simon. "A Lemon for the Teacher," The Spectator, 7004, September 21, 1962, p. 410.

The embodiment of indeterminate identity meets Rational Man and Rational Woman, yielding a "novel of ideas" which is "a statement of classic pessimism." The confrontation is riddled with pathos. "Nature is the enemy of Reason. Jake is a natural force for disorder and disaster; he refuses, he is by nature unable to work out and adopt a coherent moral position; he just wanders around, like a poltergeist, incapable of choice but spoiling for mischief. When he comes up against a delicate and rationally constructed way of life, as represented, despite all its faults by Joe and Rennie's marriage, he proceeds to smash it--casually, inevitably, without meaning to do harm any more than he means to do good."

B32 Richardson, Maurice. "Upper Crusts," New Statesman, 64, 1645 (September 21, 1962), 370-71.

Jacob Horner is suffering from "that fashionable

metaphysical disorder, a crisis of identity." Joe Morgan is "a simpleton." Barth is apparently trying to create tragic-farce like Céline but failing. His imagination lags; his language is "strange"; and he "too often falls between the stools of the maniac picaresque and the metaphysical."

B33 "Strife and Struggle," Times Literary Supplement, Sep-
       temper 28, 1962, p. 757.

"Mr. Barth applies a doctored sickness to a world of third-rate American academics whose vision of their own lives is clouded by imperfectly understood notions of physical and mental therapy...." Joe Morgan's very human contradiction of his own espoused ends has real dramatic potential but is smothered in "a dull mire of repetitive, self-examining conversations." Horner's putative lack of direction and strength is never convincing because he in fact shows himself capable of quite resolute and efficient action. The passive anti-hero is "an all too familiar creation of young novelists whose sense of dominant futility is inspired more by literature than life."

B34 "A Study in Nihilism," Time, 72, 3 (July 21, 1958),
       80.

"In describing the doctor's manifold therapies, Novel-ist Barth shows a true satirist's hatred for all the quackery visited by blind belief in the healing powers of science upon muddled, addled and wicked souls." Jacob Horner's "true calling" is "an absolute rather than a theoretical nihilism." He goes on a "one-man campaign to stamp out mental health." The novel is almost on the level of Mary Mc-Carthy's The Groves of Academe or Randall Jarrell's Pictures from an Institution. "Barth is clearly one of the most interesting of younger U.S. writers and he has produced that rarity of U.S. letters--a true novel of ideas."

B35 Wermuth, Paul C. "Barth, John. The End of the
       Road," Library Journal, 83, 15 (September 1, 1958),
       2319-20.

"The plot sounds absurd, but beneath the comic sur-face, questions are being raised regarding choice and mean-ing in life. The writing is very good, but may occasionally shock some readers."

THE SOT-WEED FACTOR

B36   Arthur, Helen. "The Marathon Adventures of a 17th-
       Century Englishman," New York Herald Tribune
       Lively Arts and Book Review, January 22, 1961,
       Section 4, p. 30.

       "This reader finds Mr. Barth and 'The Sot-Weed
Factor' talented but unco-ordinated, precious, repetitive, and
(I am certainly being repetitive myself) too long, too long,
too long."

B37   Baines, Nancy. Cape Times (Capetown, South Africa),
       November 29, 1969, p. 12.

B38   Bannon, Barbara. "The Sot-Weed Factor," Publishers
       Weekly, 190 (November 14, 1966), 111.

       The book is an "exuberant Rabelaisian satire on the
big, swashbuckling historical novel."

B39   Barker, Shirley. "History Is Still Good Fiction," Sat-
       urday Review, November 26, 1960, pp. 21-22.

       The Sot-Weed Factor is "either uproariously funny
or simply too strong for the stomach, depending on the taste
of the individual reader."

B40   "Barth, John. The Sot-Weed Factor," Choice, 4, 4
       (June 1967), 418.

       Barth has edited the original version of his novel in
order to make it more streamlined. The reader is advised
to stay with the first rendition.

B41   "The Black Humorists," Time, 85, 7 (February 12,
       1965), 94-96.

       In a survey which includes Purdy, Friedman, Heller,
Donleavy and others, Barth is represented by The Sot-Weed
Factor, which "is in no real sense a historical novel; instead
it creates a ribald, fully elaborated alternative world."

B42   Fiedler, Leslie. "John Barth: An Eccentric Genius,"
       New Leader, February 13, 1961, pp. 22-24; re-
       printed in Richard Kostelanetz, ed. On Contemporary

Literature (New York: Avon Books, 1969).

Barth is so immensely talented that he can afford to
be unfashionable. Thus, in The Sot-Weed Factor, he focuses on one small, unpromising portion of the country, Maryland, which "is not yet invented for our imaginations" and
dares to reproduce the bulk and, at times, even the tedium
of the popular historical novel he parodies. As always, he is
"an existentialist comedian suffering history." His novel re-
capitulates nearly all of the classic American themes: "the
comradeship of males, white and colored, always teetering
perilously close to, but never quite falling into, blatant homosexuality; sentimentalized brother-sister incest or quasi-in-
cest; the anti-heroic dreams of evasion and innocence; the
fear of the failed erection." He evokes a madness common
to American literature, and is healthily and unprogrammati-
cally pornographic. In this work, Barth has created "something closer to the 'Great American Novel' than any other
book of the last decades."

B43   Fuller, Edmund.   "The Joke Is on Mankind," New York
       Times Book Review, August 21, 1960, p. 4.

Barth need not have made his novel so long, "for
though he abounds in excellent satirical devices he is addicted
to repeating them." A rather special audience is required to
appreciate the work's anachronisms and verbal extravagances.
The Sot-Weed Factor is "a bare-knuckled satire of humanity
at large and the grandiose costume romance, done with meticu-
lous skill in imitation of such eighteenth-century picaresque
novelists as Fielding, Smollett and Sterne.   For all the vigor
of these models, we have to go back to Rabelais to match its
unbridled bawdiness and scatological mirth.   But the book is
not pornographic.   Rather than rousing to venery, Barth re-
duces human sexuality to a raucous pest and occasion of
folly....   He does sometimes cross the line to the simply ug-
ly in both act and attitude."

B44   Harding, Walter.   "An Historical Novel to End All His-
       torical Novels," Chicago Sunday Tribune Magazine of
       Books, August 21, 1960, part 4, p. 5.

The Sot-Weed Factor "so completely spoofs and satirizes the typical historical novel that no self-respecting historical novelist should ever be able to take himself seriously
again."

B45 Hicks, Granville. "Doubt Without Skepticism," Saturday Review, July 3, 1965, pp. 23-24.

It is not clear whether or not Todd Andrews is intended to be an admirable character. "Barth suggests that, although much can be said for cynicism, it is not enough." Jacob Horner is "even more ambiguous than Todd Andrews." Barth questions the values and motives by which people operate. "Nothing in life is as simple as it looks, and sex in particular is mysterious and many-sided." The Sot-Weed Factor is easily Barth's strongest work to date. It is entertaining, playfully erudite, and morally serious.

B46 Hyman, Stanley Edgar. "The American Adam," New Leader, March 2, 1964, pp. 20-21.

The Sot-Weed Factor, though too long and slow starting, is uproariously funny. In Barth's moral universe "it is public affairs that is wicked and sinful, while sex is harmless and benign." Sex is best when non-phallic, however. "Phallic sexuality is identified with sadism, and is typified by the book's pirates." Ebenezer's ignorance of the ways of the world make him an American Adam. Candide, which this work resembles, "is the archetypal American novel, as writers from Cooper to Salinger have demonstrated by rewriting it." The new American novel tends to be "a picaresque comedy of the anti-hero," and The Sot-Weed Factor is its funniest, if not most profound, example to date.

B47 "I ' Faith, 'Tis Good," Newsweek, 56, 9 (August 29, 1960), 88-89.

Barth, an adept disciple of Sterne, Rabelais, and Cervantes, has transmuted dissipated costume fiction into grand comedy. "As in all good comedies, there is a serious point which emerges from the wild vagaries and characters: The sometimes disastrous results of virtue in an unvirtuous world."

B48 "Invitation to Escape," Times Literary Supplement, October 27, 1961, p. 756.

The Sot-Weed Factor presents late 17th- and early 18th-century England and America as pre-industrial Sodom and Gomorrah. In situation, style, and outlook Barth has successfully "hauled himself back to the pre-psychological epic in which motives are fixed and taken for granted."

There is a weakness inherent in that very accomplishment, however: "our interest in the past is intimately linked to our anxiety about the present, and we expect of the writer's excursions into history an awareness of psychology, motive and social development as alien to Mr. Barth's novel as existentialism or Marxism should have been to Ebenezer Cooke."

B49 King, Francis. "Smog of the Spirit," New Statesmen, 62, 1596 (October 13, 1961), 524-25.

The Sot-Weed Factor is "a brilliant pastiche of late 17th and early 18th-century literature" which is "exceedingly enjoyable" but "specialized" in its appeal.

B50 Kostelanetz, Richard. "The Point Is That Life Doesn't Have Any Point," New York Times Book Review, June 6, 1965, pp. 3, 28, 30.

Catch-22, V., and The Sot-Weed Factor are discussed as examples of absurd fiction, a species of literature which "embodies absurdity in both the small events and the entire vision, in both subject matter and the form." The Sot-Weed Factor debunks history and, through ridiculing narrative conventions, "undercuts literature's pretensions to comprehending life." All three books belong to the American tradition of "antirealistic romance" which, in works like Huckleberry Finn, Billy Budd, and the novels of Bellow and Ellison, pits the individual against an oppressive social order. The means by which these themes are realized rather than the themes themselves are what make these works truly significant.

B51 McLaughlin, Richard. Springfield Republican, September 25, 1960, p. D4.

The Sot-Weed Factor is a "boisterously diverting farce" with a "serious moral."

B52 Murphy, Richard W. "In Print: John Barth," Horizon, 5, 3 (1963), 36-37.

The Floating Opera and The End of the Road "derive their energy from their flawed heroes--men who are constitutionally unable to feel or act but who invite action, even violence, as a vacuum invites implosion." As his third novel (Sot-Weed) attests, Barth is a proponent of anti-realistic contrivance in literature. He is quoted from interview on the current trend in fiction and the development of his own orientation.

B53   Petersen, Clarence. "The Sot-Weed Factor," under "Paperbacks: Among other new releases," Chicago Tribune Books Today, January 8, 1967, p. 9.

B54   _____. "Whoppers," under "Paperbacks," Washington Post Book World, May 18, 1969, p. 13.

     Now released in paperback, The Sot-Weed Factor is being billed as an underground best seller--"but that's the old underground of fervent and literate readers who've been passing the word, not the new underground with its connotations of abandoned restraint."

B55   Robie, Burton A. "Barth, John. The Sot-Weed Factor," Library Journal, 85, 16 (September 15, 1960), 3099.

     "Written in the true spirit and language of the Restoration literature by which it was inspired, this book is one huge, hilarious slice of the Human Comedy of life. Recommended for all literature or fiction collections."

B56   Shrapnel, Norman. "Boy's Own Boccaccio," The Guardian, October 13, 1961, p. 7.

     The Sot-Weed Factor is likely to become "a vogue novel for the autumn season among jaded sophisticates."

B57   "The Sot-Weed Factor," Kirkus, 28, 12 (June 15, 1960), 462-63.

     "While intricate, the plot is clear and full of the manners, morals and language of the period with a great display of poetic and philosophic knowledge. Echoes of Boccaccio, Cervantes, Voltaire and Rabelais are to be found in what is essentially a satire of a certain period done with care and style and learning. However, the literary models Mr. Barth has chosen give him ample scope for pornography and scatology and all the archaism will not disguise the elements and incidents of disgust and distaste which were certainly prominent in his earlier modern allegory, The End of the Road.

B58   "The Sot-Weed Factor," under "Paperbacks," Observer Weekend Review, October 10, 1965, p. 22.

The book is "a magnificent tour de force" written in "bastard Fieldingese."

B59   "The Sot-Weed Factor," under "Paperbacks: Fiction," Publishers Weekly, 195, 13 (March 31, 1969), 58.

Although scarcely an "underground" publication as its cover copy proclaims, The Sot-Weed Factor is indeed "a funny, literate novel that has long had a fervent, dedicated, intellectual readership that has given it word-of-mouth recommendation."

B60   Southern, Terry.   "New Trends and Old Hats," The Nation, 191, 17 (November 19, 1960), 380-83.

The Sot-Weed Factor is reviewed with six other novels, all of which are considered symptoms of the "American disease" of bigness.   Unlike his European colleagues, the American writer falls into his vocation without serious professional preparation and tends, therefore, to be intuitive, non-ideational, and original in his approach.   Barth's novel "presents itself as a 'historical novel,' or again, as a 'joke on historical novels,' and each guise is strong enough that the work may be, and is, read as either.   It is also, like Finnegans Wake, a proof of what cannot be done, or else the reason for no longer doing it; theoretically at least, the existence of The Sot-Weed Factor precludes any further possibility for the 'historical novel.' "

B61   Sutcliffe, Denham.   "Worth a Guilty Conscience," Kenyon Review, 23, 1 (1961), 181-84.

The Sot-Weed Factor is a book which returns bawdry (probably from the Old French "baud," meaning "merry") to our literature.   On the surface, Barth appears to imitate 17th-century style, but the impression is illusory.   Barth really wants genuinely antique flavor without pedantry.   "The aim ... is burlesque--even the apparently inordinate size is a joke.   ...   He burlesques the aged conventions of fiction-- mistaken identity, 'the search for the father,' true love, and all the rest--with merciless ingenuity.   No moral purpose is discoverable, no arcane 'significance,' simply fun."

B62   "The Virgin Laureate," Time, 76, 10 (September 5, 1960), 77.

Ebenezer Cooke is "one of the most diverting heroes

to roam the world since Candide." He shares a number of
parallels with Voltaire's protagonist. The novel itself is
"that rare literary creation--a genuinely serious comedy."

B63 Walsh, William J. "Barth, John: The Sot-Weed Fac-
     tor," Best Sellers, 20 (September 15, 1960), 200-01.

It is questionable whether the rewards of reading this
book offer an adequate return on the time one must invest.
"John Barth, it must be said, writes with admirable lucidity
and verve, but the range of his interests and the choice of
effects are sufficiently specialized to limit any recommendation of the book to those mature readers whose sensibilities
are not unduly shaken by the Rabelaisian approach to man's
folly."

GILES GOAT-BOY

B64 Balliett, Whitney. "Books: Rub-a-Dub-Dub," New
     Yorker, December 10, 1966, pp. 234-36.

"The book outfoxes itself. It is nothing less than an
attempt to 'spoof' the last twenty-five hundred years of Western civilization, but since history is an abstraction it tilts at
air. It is an allegory whose symbolism is embarrassingly
transparent and heavy-handed. Its characters, all of them
parodies of the famous or the infamous, of the living and the
dead, have no breath and spirit of their own.... It is a nihilistic novel with a sentimental ending."

B65 "Barth, John. Giles Goat-Boy; or, The Revised New
     Syllabus," Choice, 3, 8 (October 1966), 632.

Barth's new novel will be "a mother lode for exegetes"
for many years to come. "Swift and Nabokov are two writers
who come to mind as comparisons both to Barth's cool sav-
agery and incomparable use of language. It is almost a great
novel."

B66 Beagle, Peter S. "John Barth: Long Reach, Near
     Miss," Holiday, 40, 3 (September 1966), 131-35.

Giles Goat-Boy is a magnificent failure. In his admirable attempt to write a truly great book, Barth is be-
trayed by his own intellectualism. There are simply too
many arguments. "Slowly, though it remains fun to read,

though the ideas continue nagging and the writing inventive,
the book becomes a bore." The characters are too exclusively representational. "The people of Giles Goat-Boy
struggle to transcend their state as symbols, but they never
do; the idea is too much for them."

B67 "Black Bible," Time, 88, 6 (August 5, 1966), 92.

       Giles Goat-Boy is "a satire of major import."
George parallels Christ in many ways. "Barth's parable is
something like Dante's, a pilgrimage within an invented cos-
mology." The manner and prose sometimes approximate
those of Swift. Barth's prime concern is with "myth and religion, with the divine and the animal in man." The book, a
"black Bible," leads "not to revelation but to further mysti-
fication." As in his earlier writing, Barth "seems to say
that anything can be true if it is in the nature of the believer
to believe it so."

B68 Booklist, 63 (November 15, 1966), 363.

B69 Burgess, Anthony. "Caprine Messiah," Spectator, 218,
    7240 (March 31, 1967), 369-70.

       The Sot-Weed Factor, which operated on the assump-
tion that the novel was dead and therefore mocked both its
own subject matter and itself, suggested "one direction the
novel might take in order to progress or stay alive, which
is the same thing." Giles Goat-Boy goes even farther, implying that "now the form must revert to its mixed origins
and mock even those." It is a very big and, in that sense,
very American book. One is impressed more by the concept than by the execution, and yet "the concept is available
to any clever undergraduate."

B70 Byrd, Scott. "Giles Goat-Boy Visited," Critique, 9, 1
    (1967), 108-12.

       Barth has attempted "nothing less than an example
of Frye's 'fifth and quintessential form'--a scripture or a
sacred book." By beginning the RNS [Revised New Syllabus]
with a parodic discrepancy between the mature narrative
voice and the naive actions and perceptions of the protagonist, and then progressively closing that gap, Barth is able to
use "the confessional mode" as "a means of placing the
book's focus almost constantly on the hero and for shifting
the reader's attitude from mockery to acceptance of this

hero." He employs romance, science fiction, and an "anatomy of heroism" to address universal and contemporary aspects of the problem of "dissociation of sensibility." George is faced with the two great romantic challenges: "the conscious attack on the machine and the unconscious attack on the father." Through his failure to transform the fundamental situation, we learn that, for Barth, "a hero is not always a savior." The postscript controversy indicates that Barth was intimidated by "his audacity in creating a sacred book" and chose to retreat into ambiguity.

B71 Corbett, Edward P. J. "Giles Goat-Boy," under "Book Reviews," America, 115, 12 (September 17, 1966), 290-91.

Giles Goat-Boy is immensely rich both in story and in allegory. It is at times hard to follow because Barth, perhaps intentionally, is vague about time and space dimensions. "One never has a clear idea of where anything is taking place, or what it looks like, or how much time an action takes, or how much time elapses between events." Although the book is occasionally boring, Barth's inventiveness and verbal ability are truly impressive. The novel "may very well establish Barth as one of the three or four best contemporary American novelists." In paperback, it may become as big a campus hit as Catch-22.

B72 Corke, Hilary. "New Novels," The Listener, 77, 1983 (March 30, 1967), 437.

An author's chances of success are usually in inverse proportion to the length of his work, but "occasionally a writer occurs who can construct a single colossal super-incident that takes a quarter of a million not-a-word-wasted words to recount. Thomas Mann was one such. With Giles Goat-Boy succeeding The Sot-Weed Factor, I am left in no doubt that John Barth is another."

B73 Davis, Douglas M. "Mr. Barth Is a Grand Tease in the Rippling and Rolling 'Giles,'" National Observer, 5, 31 (August 1, 1966), 19.

"Giles Goat-Boy is sure to make Mr. Barth, till now a novelist's novelist only, at least an underground celebrity of sorts."

B74 Donoghue, Denis. "Grand Old Opry," New York Review

of Books, 7, 2 (August 13, 1966), 25-26.

Barth's principle of construction is "operatic." His books, like vaudeville shows, function as a series of discrete, more or less entertaining segments, not as organic wholes. "He is remarkably gifted in the word, the phrase, the line, but often insecure in the large economy." Barth's career is promising but uneven. "The Floating Opera is an extremely interesting first book and The Sot-Weed Factor is a remarkable achievement. But The End of the Road is not good, and Giles Goat-Boy, sprightly in rare paragraphs, is too long, too tedious, a dud."

B75 Featherstone, Joseph. "John Barth as Jonathan Swift," New Republic, September 3, 1966, pp. 17-18.

Giles Goat-Boy is "a 710-page epic snooze." This, probably the result of Barth's having spent too much time in a university setting, is extremely unfortunate, since Barth is "a comic genius" who has previously produced "an interesting novel, The Floating Opera (1956), a poor novel, End of the Road (1958), and a masterpiece, The Sot-Weed Factor (1960)."

B76 Fremont-Smith, Eliot. "The Surfacing of Mr. Barth [Laughter]," under "Books of the Times," New York Times, 115 (August 3, 1966), 35.

Barth is clearly a genius, but the implications of that fact are ambiguous: "(1) to recognize the genius, one must indulge the pedant; (2) John Barth is a pedant." The best solution is to enjoy his work without troubling one's self unduly about its ultimate significance.

B77 Garis, Robert. "Barth Defended" (letter to the editor), Commentary, 43, 1 (January 1967), 20. [See item C12.]

"Mr. Solow has caught me out fairly and embarrassingly. As for what he and the other correspondents [Howard Goldberg, Harry Lawton, and Allan J. Tobin] offer in the way of interpretation or assessment of Barth, it seems to me that none of it brings any serious question against the points I made, which still seem to me to be the central ones."

B78 "Giles Goat-Boy," Kirkus, 34, 11 (June 1, 1966), 550.

"Mr. Barth's grandiose novel is constructed as an

elaborate Conceit: the World is a University." George "emerges from his Odyssey with a Zen-like philosophy of the cyclic futility of progress, the unteachability of wisdom.... There is erudite word-wit here, a fertility of ideas that is almost febrile, a colossal serio-comic point of view, big, bawdy and boisterous. Barth plays a Swiftian game ambitiously. But it runs on and on and on. His major conceit, finally, is the assumption that the reader will tolerate almost anything for an intolerable length of time merely because it is awfully philosophical and terribly clever."

B79 "Giles Goat-Boy," under "Around the Arts: Recent and Readable," National Observer, 5, 35 (August 29, 1966), 17.

Barth's novel is "the most talked about book of the summer."

B80 "Giles Goat-Boy," Newsweek, December 19, 1966, p. 117A.

"Only a novelist of Barth's outrageous and prodigal gifts could have brought off this mad comic epic."

B81 "Giles Goat-Boy," Publishers Weekly, 191, 26 (June 26, 1967), 68.

Reviewers have varied in their response to Giles Goat-Boy, but the book has sold 50,000 copies in hardback and was distributed by two major book clubs. The paperback edition will receive a full promotional push.

B82 "Giles Goat-Boy," under "Notes on Current Books," Virginia Quarterly Review, 43, 1 (1967), viii.

In this demanding new work Barth has "revolutionized the novel form in structure, style, and content." He makes no concessions to the inexpert reader. "Mr. Barth is clearly a writer of superior quality, bewildering in the profusion of his manifest talents, and confounding in the magnitude of his vision and the depth of his intelligence."

B83 Goldberg, Howard. "Barth Defended" (letter to the editor), Commentary, 43, 1 (January 1967), 16, 20. [See item C12.]

Robert Garis's classification of Giles Goat-Boy allows

him to avoid dealing with it on its own terms. Furthermore, he misjudges the intention of Barth's allegory. "The Doctrine is not intended as a revelation to the reader, because Barth does not pretend to be the new Messiah. Rather, it is there to clothe Barth's statement that man is incapable of receiving any new doctrine because of his spiritual blindness and moral impotence."

B84 Green, Martin. "Acting the Goat," Manchester Guardian Weekly, 96, 14 (April 6, 1967), 11.

Barth, who is preoccupied with the theme of the split self, writes in the tradition of Joyce, Sterne, and Swift, but his enormous (and enormously clever) constructs finally have no serious point to make.

B85 Harding, Walter. "Barth, John. Giles Goat-Boy; or, The Revised New Syllabus," Library Journal, 91, 14 (August 1966), 3762.

"John Barth has been one of the young American authors to watch." The Sot-Weed Factor fulfilled the promise of his two earlier novels. Giles Goat-Boy "is a lengthy satire on present-day impersonalized universities and our computerized, sex-oriented lives. ... Incidents here and there are hilarious. But unfortunately what would have made a good novella has been stretched out over more than 700 pages and falls of its own weight."

B86 _____. "Satire with a Ba-a-a," Chicago Tribune Books Today, July 31, 1966, p. 3.

After the Sot-Weed Factor, Giles Goat-Boy comes as "an anti-climax." The humor and satire are often effective, often, indeed, brilliant, but the book is simply too long. "If it had been condensed to a novella, there would have been great improvement."

B87 "Heroic Comedy," Newsweek, August 8, 1966, pp. 81-82.

Giles Goat-Boy "confirms Barth's standing as perhaps the most prodigally gifted comic novelist writing in English today."

B88 Hicks, Granville. "Crowned with the Shame of Men," Saturday Review, August 6, 1966, pp. 21-23.

Giles Goat-Boy is a "philosophical novel" which runs counter to the prevailing American tradition of non-intellectual fiction. "If I say that Barth has used his intellect, it is not because I am ready to accept all his answers--I'm not even sure what some of them are--but because I think he has dared to ask himself the right questions." The book is infinitely rich, both in detail and in scope. "If this isn't a great success, as at the moment I think, it is a great failure. One way or the other, there is greatness in it."

B89 Hill, William B. "Giles Goat-Boy," under "Fiction,"
America, 115, 22 (November 26, 1966), 706-07.

"A strange and really compelling book, an intelligent, witty parable, penetrating, by turns reverent and blasphemous, scatological to the point of being scandalous, Swiftian except for its verbosity." The final meaning of George's message seems to be " 'live and be human.' "

B90 Johnson, B. S. Books and Bookmen, 12 (April 1967),
60.

B91 "The Joker Is Wild," Times Literary Supplement,
March 30, 1967, p. 261.

Giles Goat-Boy is a monumental allegory, the academic novel to end all academic novels, and an oblique commentary on contemporary politics. "But neither the inner key of this allegory nor the outer key of the contemporary charade is what ultimately matters.... It is freedom for the human being to be fully human that matters.... In that sense, the allegory is perhaps ultimately meant as a parable whose challenge is to apply our judgment to life." The grand edifice is unfortunately built on an insufficient central metaphor. The comedy succeeds. "But to treat the university as a paradigm of the universe is in itself capricious. Whatever this may reveal about universities, it is not at all revealing about the universe."

B92 Kitching, Jessie. "Giles Goat-Boy," Publishers Weekly,
189, 21 (May 23, 1966), 81.

The novel is "at once earthy and symbolic," conveying "a satiric vision of bickering mankind," and is a "universal rather than merely political satire."

B93 Klein, Marcus. "Gods and Goats," The Reporter, 35,

4 (September 22, 1966), 60-62.

"The book is monumental and imposing, and the comedy, after the manner of heroism, is awesomely impersonal." Barth began his career by positing "the ultimate metaphysical horror: there is no reason for anything." Ever since, his protagonists have struggled with the very terms of being. "In all Barth's fiction, existence--nothing less--is the enemy." All idealism must be tested against the realities of a world "diseased, perverted, malodorous, gummy with the detritus of ordinary human lives." All Barth's previous books have culminated in submission of one sort or another. In Giles Goat-Boy, he attempts a "reconciliation" and finds that life's apparent polarities are in fact "circular and interpenetrating." The ending suffers from being too much the result of merely allegorical formulation, but it has the virtue of implying that the struggle for resolution is both perpetually necessary and necessarily perpetual.

B94   Kostelanetz, Richard.   " 'The New American Fiction'
       Reconsidered," Triquarterly, 8 (1967), 279-86.

Giles Goat-Boy, though "hardly as great as The Sot-Weed Factor," is nevertheless "a first-rate book, surely among the dozen or so best novels of the passing sixties." It lacks "the conspicuously eye-catching writing and the natural comic energy" of its predecessor. As a character, the goat-boy is "by design too innocent to give the novel the consistently comic tone its plot needs." The jokes are excessive in number, do not grow naturally out of their situations, and are at odds with the tragic ending. The work is an attempt at "historical parable" in the manner of Animal Farm, and may be intended as "a satirical history of Christianity." The analogues to contemporary phenomena do not "rise easily out of the fiction, " and, as insights, "they are practically meaningless." Barth, with his stupendous gift of style and penchant for "the comedy of excessive complication, " sometimes overwrites. Like Melville, Faulkner, and Fitzgerald before him, he may find that "he has published his masterpiece at the age of thirty. "

B95   Lawton, Harry.   "Barth Defended" (letter to the editor),
       Commentary, 43, 1 (January 1967), 20.   [See item
       C12.]

Robert Garis has read Giles Goat-Boy on the level of superstructure only, where it must appear as mere science fiction. "Only when one looks below the surface icing is it clear that Barth has opposed a Christian superstructure to a pagan substructure." The title suggests "not only St. Giles, patron saint of cripples ... but the Greek derivation of Aegis, the shield made from the goat that fostered Zeus, and also Aegisthus, the Greek hero raised among goats...." Lord Raglan's The Hero furnishes the information necessary for an understanding of the book. Giles is associated most closely with Oedipus and even fulfills the riddle of the Sphinx "by walking first on four legs as a goat, then on two and finally on three legs (holding a staff) as he enters the University."

B96   Levitas, Gloria. "City Blights," under "Paperbacks," Washington Post Book World, September 17, 1967, p. 15.

Giles Goat-Boy "convinces us that it was written by the computer whose civilization it purports to satirize. Barth's comic gifts are not sufficient to sustain this agglutinated tour-de-force of sophomoric humor, theological fantasy and leering sex. Novels, like civilizations, cannot be created by intellectual machines."

B97   McColm, Pearlmarie. "The Revised New Syllabus and the Unrevised Old," Denver Quarterly, 1, 3 (1966), 136-41.

"John Barth's recent tour-de-farce is an ambitious mock satire, a distended myth, and an epic pasquinade which occasionally reads a little like Dr. Johnson, occasionally like Swift, and most often like Rabelais." Giles Goat-Boy does not really succeed as a satire because "the parallels are more often verbal--funny, but superficial--than they are politically or socially vigilant." Barth claims that the realistic novel is perhaps growing dated, yet "he adopts an out-of-date story-telling method to satirize form itself." He thereby demands the "willing suspension of realistic values" and thus satirizes the reader himself.

B98   MacNamara, Desmond. "Scape Goat," New Statesman, 73, 1881 (March 31, 1967), 442.

Giles Goat-Boy is the Jurgen of this generation. The work is enjoyable, even worthwhile, but too long. "It could have been a savoury bonne bouche instead of a barely digestible platter of pasta."

B99   Maddocks, Melvin. Christian Science Monitor, August 4, 1966, p. 5.

Giles Goat-Boy is "a cumbersomely allegorical story which tries to save itself from the embarrassment of philosophical naivete by a heavy coverup of bawdiness."

B100   Malin, Irving. "Giles Goat-Boy," Commonweal, 85, 9 (December 2, 1966), 270.

This work "transforms the Novel as it creates the Transformed World." Barth combats the Computer, "symbol of the present or forthcoming doom."

B101   Merril, J. Magazine of Fantasy and Science Fiction, 32 (March 1967), 20.

B102   Morse, J. Mitchell. "Fiction Chronicle," Hudson Review, 19, 3 (1966), 507-14.

"Barth's Giles Goat-Boy is not so much science fiction as undergraduate humor-magazine fiction." It is trash masquerading as literature. "Plato and his followers regretted that the mind had a body; D. H. Lawrence and his followers regretted that the body had a mind; Rabelais regretted neither; Barth regrets both. ... He still thinks sex is dirty, he still likes it dirty, and he is still a relativist. His values, that is to say, are still those of a tame goat."

B103   O'Connell, Shaun. "Goat Gambit at the University," The Nation, 203, 6 (September 5, 1966), 193-95.

"Barth is a novelist of ideas who has consistently undercut the validity of basing human behavior too closely upon intellectual preconceptions." In this novel, his execution does not, unfortunately, match his intention. He seems so obsessed with "intellectual superstructure" that he neglects to create an engaging surface. We are asked to move too quickly to the level of abstract thought. "Barth, like his own heroes, over-valued ideas."

B104   Petersen, Clarence. "Giles Goat-Boy," under "Paperbacks: Among other new releases," Chicago Tribune Books Today, August 20, 1967, p. 13.

Barth's new novel has met with "mixed reviews."

B105   "Pick of the Paperbacks," Saturday Review, 50, 38
        (September 30, 1967), 46-47.

            Giles Goat-Boy is "weighty..., mystic, allegorical."
Critics have compared its protagonist to both Mephistopheles
and Batman.

B106   Poirier, Richard. "Wescac and the Messiah," Chi-
        cago Sun-Times [and other newspapers'] Book Week
        August 7, 1966, pp. 1, 12.

            Barth's latest novel contributes to the impression
that the post-World War II period is one of the richest in our
literary history. This is due, in part, to the fact that our
novelists, taking their cue from Joyce and from their own
French contemporaries, have discovered a wealth of new material in the novel itself. Much of the life in Barth's work
is "digressive," an expression of "existential liberty." His
method works best over the short haul--in paragraphs,
scenes, short novels--because elaborating systems only to
undermine them is "unnourishing and repetitious" once the
principle is grasped. The book's blatant allegorical element
reminds us that, given the nature of human understanding,
we necessarily live in "an allegorical dream world." The
point is not so much to sort out the correspondences as to
perceive the significance of the encoding itself. "The implication is that the human imagination, out of which all these
have issued, is impossibly entangled in its own creations and
that it gets even more entangled by efforts to put experience
into exclusive or merely orderly categories."

B107   "Samplings," Teachers College Record, 68, 2 (Novem-
        ber 1966), 185-86.

            "The book is vast and comic and sometimes puzz-
ling. Echoes of the whole world's history and literature are
summoned up, even as the reader is thrust back into the consciousness of his own fragile self at the center of a computerized world."

B108   Samuels, Charles Thomas. "John Barth: A Bouyant
        Denial of Relevance," Commonweal, 85, 3 (October
        21, 1966), 80-82.

            Barth's first two books illustrate why he is little
read despite his enthusiastic critical reception. "Their characters are dialectic sticks dressed in the thinnest of psycho-

logical garments.... The plots through which they mechani-
cally move are inorganic, since such characters cannot project themselves through action but only through talk. Barth
relies on rhetoric, or rhetoric sliced into dialogue to convey
a liveliness, as this device avows, which is intellectual if it
is anything. Disappointingly, the ideas in both books are
banal." The Sot-Weed Factor is marred by over-complexity,
a self-consciously "worked-up salaciousness," and a style
that has "the vulgar ease of aimless imitation." Giles Goat-
Boy employs "the oldest, leakiest, most cumbersome of devices: allegory." The long, childish game dissipates
through the various posttapes into "an affirmation of meaninglessness, madness, ungovernable flux." Barth's sniggering
attitude is a negation of the very basis of art. "Beneath
Barth's novels and the taste which finds them congenial is a
laughing denial of relevance, accuracy, even truth."

B109   Schlueter, Paul. "Puncturing the Gods," Christian
        Century, 83, 38 (September 21, 1966), 1149.

        Barth manages to satirize at least three major
areas at once--academia, technology, and human nature.
There can be no doubt that Giles Goat-Boy is "one of the important books of the year" and that Barth is "one of this
country's most gifted writers in language and in imagination."

B110   Scholes, Robert. " 'George Is My Name,' " New
        York Times Book Review, August 7, 1966, pp. 1,
        22.

        Giles Goat-Boy is a great novel. Its supremacy is
most apparent in "its striking originality of structure and language, an originality that depends upon a superb command of
literary and linguistic tradition rather than an eccentric manipulation of the 'modern.' " The achievement, along with
that of The Sot-Weed Factor, identifies Barth as "the best
writer of fiction we have at present, and one of the best we
have ever had." The structure of Giles involves "a double
quest: the traditional heroic journey of the awkward knight
who combats evil, rescuing a damsel and slaying a dragon in
pursuit of a divine object; and the modern search for identity
of the existential anti-hero." The dragon turns out to be internal and personal--"a demon of the absolute, which drives
him toward either/or solutions in a world which is not amen-
able to them." The book both demands and amply rewards
readers prepared by tradition and by the great modern
writers. "Barth is a comic genius of the highest order."

B111   Schott, Webster. "A Black Comedy to Offend Every-
        one," Life, 61, 7 (August 12, 1966), 10.

        Barth's new novel spoils the attempt that was being
made to convert him into a cult figure. "Long, boring, frustrating, Giles Goat-Boy cultivates tedium. Its only mitigating
quality is Barth's wild originality." The protagonist "winds
up in an insane asylum/power house, a terminal neurotic and
founder of a crazy sect." In the process of getting him there,
Barth manages to confuse all moral categories. "Giles Goat-
Boy is the novel with something to offend everyone....
Barth's misanthropic outrage and novel fascination with ambiguity take priority over all those other things we prize in
fiction. He develops no characters. He creates no drama.
He finds no emotional ranges and searches no human depths.
Barth bets everything on attack, and he loses. He loses because, to succeed, satire must identify values. It must imply through negation the properties it esteems and seeks to
commemorate through absurd and ironic representations.
Barth's University is limbo inhabited by idiotic idealists and
glorious devils. It celebrates death. The Cold War is for
kicks."

B112   Shapiro, Joel L. "Barth, John: Giles Goat-Boy,"
        Best Sellers, 26 (October 1, 1966), 231-32.

        This book substantiates the current estimation of
John Barth as a writer "in the forefront of contemporary
'greats' of American Literature." But the attempt to "represent the total fabric of human existence and interplay" renders the work intimidating. "The book's themes are as varie-
gated as life itself and while parts of it will hold any reader
with compelling force, its entirety will be palatable only to
those who take it up as a 'project'.... Perhaps it will be
some future generation's 'Ulysses,' but for now this reviewer
will place it on his shelf with a resigned sigh of relief."

B113   Shuttleworth, Martin. "New Novels," Punch, 252,
        6604 (April 5, 1967), 504.

        Giles Goat-Boy is creaking and cleverly mechanical.
"On and on he goes, playful, winsome, gusty, blissfully una-
ware that no academic who respects neither life nor suffering
has ever broached a cracker barrel of his own, however much
he may know of other people's."

B114   Solow, Martin. "Barth Defended" (letter to the editor),

Commentary, 43, 1 (January 1967), 16. [See item C12.]

In correcting a putative error in the New York Times Book Review, Robert Garis himself mistakenly attributed the journal in question to Captain James Smith instead of Captain John Smith. "As for the Sot-Weed Factor, I think it is just about the best novel written in the United States since Moby Dick. Because it teems with satire, comedy, richness, boldness, and depth of language, it may have been a bit too overwhelming for a man who prefers the fleshless, drained, cerebral prose of Nabokov."

B115   Stuart, Dabney. "A Service to the University," Shenandoah, 18, 1 (1966), 96-99.

Giles Goat-Boy raises the problem of whether or not the book itself is a novel; continues Barth's concern with "illusion, deception, masks"; questions "the reality or unreality of distinctions"; elaborates further on the issue of twinship raised in The Sot-Weed Factor; utilizes the devices of parody and allegory; and manifests a circular progress. In terms of worth, the book "ranks with Moby Dick as the best fiction yet written by an American."

B116   Tobin, Allan J. "Barth Defended" (letter to the editor), Commentary, 43, 1 (January 1967), 16. [See item C12.]

Robert Garis is evidently a pedant intent on spoiling the reading enjoyment of others. "The fact that a non-lover of Swift unfavorably compares Barth to Swift is hardly an interesting basis for criticism of two provocative and totally entertaining novels."

LOST IN THE FUNHOUSE

B117   Adams, Phoebe. "Lost in the Funhouse," under "Short Reviews: Books," The Atlantic, 222, 4 (October 1968), 150.

The title story "includes amusing experiments, Homeric excursions, and the revelation that Mr. Barth can write verse just like that of the late Rudyard Kipling."

B118   Appel, Alfred, Jr. "The Art of Artifice," The Nation,

207, 14 (October 28, 1968), 441-42.

Barth has produced a series of "involuted" stories.
"An involuted work turns in upon itself, is self-referential
and conscious of its status as invention.   An ideally involuted sentence would simply read, 'I am a sentence,' and
Barth's 'Title' and 'Life-Story' come as close to this dubious
ideal as any fiction can."   Barth is one of the most successful members of the second generation of post-modernists--
those writers for whom Beckett, Borges, and Nabokov have
succeeded Joyce, Proust, and Kafka as creative models.

B119   Ardery, P. P.   National Review, 20 (December 3,
          1968), 1230.

B120   Axthelm, Pete.   "Tiny Odyssey," Newsweek, 72, 14
          (September 30, 1968), 106-07.

Lost in the Funhouse records an artist's odyssey
"with images borrowed from Homer, and heroes and word-
play derived from Joyce."

B121   "Barth, John.   Lost in the Funhouse," Choice, 6
          (April 1969), 210.

B122   Cassils, R. V.   "The Artist As Art," Washington
          Post Book World, 2, 37 (September 15, 1968), 16.

The book is gimmicky, although it must be said
that, at his best, Barth is "an entertaining gimmicker." He
goes astray and produces a "blitheringly sophomoric book"
because he falls victim to "the vulgar notion that art, life
and their vocabularies really are distinct and that you make
art out of life by talking about it in 'an original way.' "

B123   Davenport, Guy.   "Like Nothing Nameable," New York
          Times Book Review, October 20, 1968, pp. 4, 63.

"In his new and thoroughly confusing work of fiction
John Barth seems at first blush to be like a great architect
making a batch of doll houses just to show that his virtuosity
includes mastery over the elegant trifle and the deft sketch."
Having displayed complete command of literary conventions in
his earlier novels, Barth has now set about challenging those
very conventions with alternatives that owe much to the influence of Beckett and McLuhan.   He is such an inveterate
storyteller, however, that he produces solidly readable stories

despite himself. "His real interest is in the reader and in the metaphysical plight of imagination engaging with imagination." He makes us tremendously aware that, although fiction may be only so much "tushery," the world "has been in love with it for several millennia, never quite aware what it is."

B124   "Fables for People Who Can Hear with Their Eyes," Time, 92, 13 (September 27, 1968), 100.

Like Proteus, Barth "keeps his artistic assets as liquid as possible." Lost in the Funhouse is "a work of highly significant irrelevance."

B125   Fenton, James. "Barthist," New Statesman, 78, 2010 (September 19, 1969), 384-85.

Lost in the Funhouse is "a fascinating and highly entertaining work." John Barth is "surely one of the most brilliant and inventive writers of our time."

B126   Garis, Robert. "Fiction Chronicle," The Hudson Review, 22, 1 (1969), 148-164 [especially 163-64].

There may be significant relationships between the Ambrose stories and the more experimental pieces, but it is just as likely that "the structural pretensions are pure put-on." Fortunately, Barth has recovered the authentically funny voice that was long imprisoned in The Sot-Weed Factor and Giles Goat-Boy. The voice is precisely what makes this new volume a joy.

B127   Harding, Walter. "Barth, John. Lost in the Funhouse," under "Fiction," Library Journal, 93, 16 (September 15, 1968), 3153.

The Ambrose stories are best. "A series of experimental pieces on the art of writing will appeal to students of fiction. But a group of pseudo-Homeric tales are as bloated and over-written as the worst parts of Giles Goat-Boy. In all, a mixed bag varying from some of the best works to come from Barth's very talented pen to some of the poorest."

B128   Harper, Howard M., Jr. "Trends in Recent American Fiction," Contemporary Literature, 12, 1 (1971), 204-29 [especially 210-11].

Lost in the Funhouse is "less ambitious" than
Giles Goat-Boy but "more personal and moving." Many people have found Barth's previous work "too cold, too cerebral,
too clever, too self-conscious." This book portrays an artist aware of those qualities in himself and struggling to over-
come them. Worlds of "profound human dimensions" are
created within the volume. "The fact that the narrators are
able to enter those worlds only through the use of technical
expertise is a sad but profoundly true comment on contemporary man and his civilization."

B129   Hicks, Granville. "The Up-to-Date Looking Glass,"
           Saturday Review, 51 (September 28, 1968), 31-32.

In Lost in the Funhouse, Barth has "tried to renew
the art of fiction by making use of allegory, fantasy, and
symbol." The shallow experiments of shallow talents must
not be held against the innovative attempts of real artists.
"Barth has proved again and again that he can equal the tra-
ditionalists at their own game, and thus he has won the right
to be different." Giles Goat-Boy now seems in retrospect
"one of the most important novels of our time." Though
some of its experiments appear unproductive, Lost in the
Funhouse is "further evidence that Barth has a first-rate imagination."

B130   Hill, William B. "Lost in the Funhouse," under
           "Fiction," America, 119, 18 (November 30, 1968),
           563-64.

"Too much has been made of the oral-aural nature
of the pieces in this collection. Actually they can be read
simply, silently, happily. They are not John Barth at his
best, but he is, as always, compelling in these narratives
that are a revelation of youth and the wooing of the muses.
They are frightfully allusive."

B131   Hjortsberg, William. "John Barth in the Global Vil-
           lage," Catholic World, 208, (January 1969), 188.

In this work, "Barth exhibits his astonishing verbal
legerdemain in an array of stories that vary radically in
technique yet manage to achieve a distinct sense of unity."
The Moebius strip effectively frames the whole, while "Night-
Sea Journey" "mirrors obliquely the final 'Anonymiad.' "
The experiments designed for tape are less adventurous than
those designed for print. Barth is one writer who can feel

comfortably at home in McLuhan's global village.

B132   Hood, Stuart. "Silver-Age Fun," The Listener, 82,
            2112 (September 18, 1969), 385.

        "The book itself is a funhouse erected by a writer
who appears ... to believe that the novel is a fag-end of tradition and we are members of a rundown civilisation." The
writer's stance is like that of "a decadent author of the
classical age."   He uses myths "to act out the inner dramas
of the artist."   Barth's fictional funhouse is not without its
difficulties, but "there are extraordinary things to be found
there."

B133   "Just for the Record," Times Literary Supplement,
            3525 (September 18, 1969), 1017.

        The Ambrose stories are the best of the lot.
"Here at last, Barth can forget the blank page, the dotted
line, the regressus in infinitum of artifice.   Like Lewis
Carroll's, like Nabokov's, his finest logical fantasies take
wing from experience--on the Maryland seashore, or outings
to Ocean City."

B134   Lemon, Lee T.   "Barth's Good Book," Prairie
            Schooner, 43, 2 (1969), 231-32.

        The work is "a kind of hodge-podge that hangs to-
gether only by the grace of Barth's persistent vision of the
overly sensitive man." If the book can be said to have a
central theme, it is "the implication of being a creator."
The creator's dilemma springs from the opposition of his
hunger for full participation in life and his sense of destined
exclusion.   Despite Barth's disclaimers, Lost in the Funhouse succeeds perfectly well when read by the eye alone;
and it coheres, for all its fragmentation, into "an extremely
good book."

B135   "Lost in the Funhouse," Kirkus, 34, 15 (August 1,
            1968), 836.

        "No American writer under forty is as lavishly ad-
mired as John Barth." He "can do everything except create
characters or a psychological terrain capable of truly draw-
ing the reader into his intricate designs....   Thus he is not
at his best in this uneven and randomly connected collection
of short stories.   A number of the pieces seem to be failed

excursions on philosophical themes which have perhaps been excised from longer works, while others are modishly experimental.... The title-story, a surprisingly fairly conventional memory of the adolescent Id, is quite fine, even moving in its sprightly way, and should, unlike the others, stand the test of time."

B136   "Lost in the Funhouse," Publishers Weekly, 194, 5 (July 29, 1968), 56.

"Barth experiments wildly and at will with fictional forms, often commenting on the fact as he goes, and there are moments when it all seems like something of a pretentious put-on. That's probably unfair, but, in the end, the results are more curious than rewarding or successful."

B137   "Lost in the Funhouse," under "Notes on Current Books: Fiction," Virginia Quarterly Review, 45, 4 (1969), cxxviii.

"As experimental prose or structure, this volume will not change the course of American letters; but there is much good writing, much good humor, and a great deal of interest, just what we have come to expect from Barth. When he becomes philosophical his art breaks down; it is the philosophy of 1940 Existentialism, and is painfully dated. But when he is telling a story few in the country can match him."

B138   Magazine of Fantasy and Science Fiction, 36 (January 1969), 40.

B139   Murray, John J. "Barth, John: Lost in the Funhouse," Best Sellers, 28 (October 15, 1968), 282.

"Barth is certainly a genius. He is, when style for style's sake is used as a criterion, among the best writers of these or any times. One suspects that whatever can be done with words, he can do it." The technical peculiarities of this volume parody rather than merely illustrate McLuhan's dicta.

B140   Observer, September 14, 1969, p. 29.

B141   Richardson, Jack. "Amusement and Revelation," New Republic, 159, 21 (November 23, 1968), 30-35.

After the original "seed" of "Night-Sea Journey" is planted, the stories of this volume fall into two phases, the first concerned with the development of a young writer's sensibility, the second with the ramifications of his self-identification as Author. The book very profitably forces us to reexamine "our practiced notions of reading."

B142   Schott, Webster. "One Baffled Barth in Search of a Book," Life, 65, 16 (October 18, 1968), 8.

If the "jejune" pieces of Lost in the Funhouse represent the fiction of the future, "then it's ashcan literature awaiting us. We'll be wrapping fish in books instead of newspapers." This book, as Barth must know, is "a grinding bore." Unless he is writing out of habit or vainglory, he is apparently attempting--unsuccessfully--to supersede traditional realistic friction. "New esthetic epiphany is beyond Barth's range." The best piece in the book, "Water Message," is in the very vein Barth claims is bankrupt. Barth is obviously talented. "But his education is incomplete. He must learn to fill his wastebaskets with his penmanship practice and his psychotherapeutic wanderings. He must learn to spend more time looking at the world outside his study and less time poring over the yellowing clippings in which he has promised to play Che Guevara to American letters."

B143   Tanner, Tony. "No Exit," Partisan Review, 36, 2 (1969), 293-99.

Barth has always been what Robert Musil called a "possibilitarian," and, as such, he is susceptible to what Kierkegaard labeled "the despair of possibility." In Lost in the Funhouse he has fallen victim to his own "sense of the arbitrariness of invention." In this work "he can no longer get hold of any 'reality' at all; everything he touches turns into fictions and yet more fictions." Apparently, the only reason he goes on writing at all is that "there seems to be an underlying feeling that identity is coextensive and coterminous with articulation. The 'I' is only ascertainable as that which speaks: self is voice, but voice speaking unnecessary and arbitrary and untrue words." This verbal sense of self, for all its evident unsatisfactoriness, is nevertheless preferable to the temptation of "dissolution and silence," which, like the alternative dread of fixed patterns, is a recurring nightmare for many contemporary American writers.

B144   Tube, Henry. "Vivification," Spectator, 7368 (September 13, 1969), 374-75.

Barth's voice "seems to try to make up in heartiness for what it lacks in precise feeling." The result is a kind of "spurious vividness."

CHIMERA

B145 Ackroyd, Peter. "Chinese Boxes and Other Novels,"
       The Spectator, 7621, July 20, 1974, p. 86-87.

Barth has imposed the "trifling concerns" of self-conscious craftsmanship on his readers. The first section draws upon "some pot-pourri known as the Thousand and One Nights which Mr. Barth thinks of some cross-cultural importance." The author's "intolerable urge for systems and meanings" may impress "the more unintelligent reviewers," but it is clear that he is "trying to spin gold out of the pointless questions which pursue formalists and aestheticians." The last two sections are even more disastrous because "Americans, being a poorly educated race, take the Greek myths far too seriously and become either pompous or heavily jocular about them." Barth has taken the latter approach and turned the fables into "an elaborate apologia for his own apparently miserable and wasted life."

B146 Adams, Phoebe. "Chimera," under "Short Reviews:
       Books," The Atlantic, 230, 4 (October 1972), 135.

Barth attempts to present the artist as mythic hero. "But the old tales are so overlaid with stylistic smartaleckry, plus women's lib rhetoric and lumps from Roget's Thesaurus that their principal effect is to raise echoes of Jurgen and The Private Life of Helen of Troy--two works that nobody should be asked to remember."

B147 Allen, Bruce. "Barth, John. Chimera," Library
       Journal, 97, 14 (August 1972), 2638.

"We probably should simply trust that John Barth's ambiguous position on the question of fiction's ambiguous relationship to reality is committed to the achievement of a new technique, and is probing depths through which he alone may just be beginning to see. A breakthrough seems to be near."

B148 "Barth, John. Chimera," Choice, 9, 10 (December

1972), 1288-90.

"In Chimera, Barth has grasped many experimental techniques for which he was merely reaching in Lost in the Funhouse ... and Giles Goat-Boy." He also manages to parody "the plot of his own Sot-Weed Factor (1960), the style of Nabokov, and the feminist ideas of Robert Graves." The book is as innovative as any novel since Tristam Shandy, "which it resembles." Women liberationists may find it offensive.

B149   Booklist, 69 (November 15, 1972), 274.

B150   Breslin, John B.   "A Prospect of Books," America, 127, 10 (October 7, 1972), 265.

The publication of Chimera is mentioned in a survey of the year's offerings. Barth exploits Greek legend for this "triptych."

B151   Bryant, Jerry H.   "Chimera," The Nation, 215, 20 (December 18, 1972), 631-33.

Chimera is a "simulated fiction," that is, "a lecture on the nature of fiction, disguised as the retelling of some very old stories." As such, the novel is divorced from the life and interest of the bulk of the reading public. Barth's stories "are about story telling, not about people." Their appeal, therefore, is necessarily severely limited.   "If the novel is dead, it's because intelligent writers like Barth, who could continue to re-create it, haven't found a new way to say something about the world but only a new way to say something about saying something about the world."

B152   "Chimera," Kirkus, 40, 14 (July 15, 1972), 813.

"These three long stories carry Barth dangerously near the vanishing point he has been approaching for some time--fictions turning back on themselves in ever tighter, more exquisitely esoteric loops till subject and form swallow each other up in a single abstract identity. Essentially these are experiments with narrative strategy drawn obliquely from classic models, and their recurrent theme of sexual politics seems to be a take-off from Barth's analogy for the relationship between writer and reader.   ...   If you can appreciate it there's a heroic aspect to all this: the writer braving the impossible with humor and style.   There's also something slightly eccentric about Barth's determination to do so."

B153   "Chimera," under "1972: A Selection of Noteworthy
        Titles," New York Times Book Review, December
        3, 1972, p. 74.

        "Three ancient myths ... recast in a complicated
fictional mold in which imagination and the artfully verbal
intermingle 'in pursuit of a pattern [made] in that very pursuit'--mythology shaped as fabulation."

B154   "Chimera" under "Briefly Noted: Fiction," New
        Yorker, 48 (September 30, 1972) 125.

        "All three parts of this book ... are parodies in a
quite destructive sense; they are like the doodles and wise-
cracks a schoolboy scribbles across the pages of his text-
books. Mr. Barth cannot improve on the original works; he
merely wants to remind us of his presence. He gives us
harebrained speculation about fiction and the academic life,
and (for humor) numerous jokes about sexual impotence."

B155   "Chimera," under "Briefly," Psychology Today, 6, 8
        (January 1973), 20.

        "Barth's style is a delight, but it confuses the is-
sue of where the talking should be done--in bed or in book."

B156   "Chimera," Publishers Weekly, 202, 5 (July 31, 1972),
        67.

        The first two novellas are "entertaining if one has
the taste for clever plays upon words and some knowledge of
and interest in the myths on which they are based." The
third, however, "will discourage all but the most scholarly
classicist or devout Barth fan. It seems to go interminably,
twists in and out and back on itself so much as to be almost
impenetrable, and however clever it is in certain passages,
the sheer density of the writing, the too precious eccentricity
of it all is ultimately self-defeating."

B157   "Chimera," Publishers Weekly, 204, 7 (August 13,
        1973), 57.

        The novel, which Publishers Weekly gave a mixed
review, has won the National Book Award and is being reis-
sued in paperback with educational promotion.

B158   Cresset, 36 (April 1973), 11.

B159   Crinklaw, Don. "One Low Voice in Wild Company,"
        National Review, 24, 40 (October 13, 1972), 1136-
        37.

        "Myths shaping stories shaping lives. Like the
footnotes to The Waste Land, the apparatus is there if you
want it. So, fortunately, is a fine randy comic epic. It's
a shimmering, magical book--probably the best Barth has
produced so far."

B160   Cunningham, Valentine. "Bags of Tricks," New
        Statesman, 88, 2261 (July 19, 1974), 90.

        "Chimera isn't only a shatteringly clever and scur-
rilous rewrite of some classic fictions, it's also the trickiest,
most shimmeringly elusive of reflections on the art and artifices of the novel."

B161   Deutsch, André. "The Narrative Springs," Times
        Literary Supplement, July 26, 1974, p. 783.

        Barth's latest work is an elaborate exercise in
what he once called Mythotherapy. The results are at once
impressive and exasperating: "following The Sot-Weed Factor and Giles Goat-Boy, Chimera joins a body of work which
must now be easily the best worst in modern fiction."

B162   Ellman, Mary. "Recent Novels," Yale Review, 62,
        3 (1973), 461-68 [especially 468].

        "John Barth's Chimera aspires to be comic and
mythical as well. It has to be read in snatches. In the
kindest of worlds, one would read two pages a day, in the
morning. As much as three pages a day, and the reader is
transformed into a shelf holding forty remaindered copies of
Chimera. "

B163   H., V. "Lost in the Barth-house," Christian Science
        Monitor, 64 (September 20, 1972), 10.

        " 'Chimera' continues the kind of self-reflexive
horseplay, the kind of 'look, Ma, no hands' stylistic manner-
ism that dominated Barth's last collection of pieces, called
'Lost in the Funhouse.' " Readers who enjoy such games may
find this work amusing. "There will be others, like myself,
who are waiting for Barth tu develop the considerable gifts
he displayed in 'The Floating Opera,' and who till then find

him still lost in the fiction house."

B164 Hill, William B. "<u>Chimera</u>," under "Fiction," <u>Amer-</u>
        <u>ica</u>, 127, 16 (November 18, 1972), 422.

        "This book is about as full of controlled madness
as any book is likely to be." In its concern with myth and
creativity, "Barth's work probably has more raw sex per
page than anything else that has been done recently. This
book is for a limited audience; many people would flounder
in it."

B165 Lehmann-Haupt, Christopher. "Found in the Fun-
        house," <u>New York Times</u>, 122 (September 20, 1972),
        45.

        Barth has at last overcome both the "tedious in-
dulgence" of <u>Giles Goat-Boy</u> and <u>Lost in the Funhouse</u> and
the writer's block which followed them. He attributes the
triumph to his discovery of the Principle of Metaphoric
Means. What he means by that phrase and precisely how it
applies to <u>Chimera</u> is hard to say. For the reader, the
most important point is simply that Barth has regained control of his talent and rediscovered an unabashed sense of fun.

B166 McLellan, John. "<u>Chimera</u>," under "Paperbacks:
        Fiction," <u>Washington Post Book World</u>, 7 (Novem-
        ber 18, 1973), 5.

        Barth won a National Book Award for this foray in-
to myth: "Scheherazade as a crusader for women's lib (with
someone who resembles John Barth as a genie); Perseus aging and wondering what it all means; Bellerophon assailed by
self doubt."

B167 Michaels, Leonard. "<u>Chimera</u>," <u>New York Times</u>
        <u>Book Review</u>, September 24, 1972, pp. 35-37.

        In Chimera, talking about the work is the work,
and the problem raised is that of "verbal suicide." Barth
himself stands outside the book, beyond the problem he dis-
cusses. The hero motif constitutes a bomb. "In the last
pages it is used to explode the whole book."

B168 Perkins, Bill. "In One of Three, Barth Seems Not
        So Parched and Plucked After All," <u>The National</u>
        <u>Observer</u>, 11 (October 7, 1972), 21.

After a strong beginning, Barth's career has long
been plagued by "empty explorations of narrative technique, "
"excessive rewrites of classical mythology, " and "writer's
block. " The first tale of his new work has at last provided
a format whereby those handicaps could be turned to advan-
tage. "In 'Dunyazadiad, ' Barth's most rewarding creation in
years, there is hope for his future. " With Scheherazade as
his muse, Barth "may yet become the hero that most of us
thought he could be. "

B169   Prescott, Peter S.   "Heroes Over the Hill, " News-
        week, 80 (October 9, 1972), 108.

"The substance of these enchanting stories, which
progress from youth and sex to an aging hero to an ironic
imitation of a hero's life, becomes--skillfully, deceivingly--
inseparable from the narration. "

B170   _____ .   "Readout: The Year in Books, " News-
        week, 81, 1 (January 1, 1973), 53-54.

"Good myth refers to the totality of man's condition, and so do these stories, which are concerned with sex,
ambition and the problems of aging heroes. ...   These baroque stories are funny and, in an academic way, engaging. "

B171   Sage, Lorna.   "Low Life on Olympus, " Observer Re-
        view, July 21, 1974, p. 27.

Chimera intentionally exposes the devices other novels attempt to conceal.   "Reading is a conscious process
again, rather like suddenly having to count on your fingers. "
Like Philip Roth, Barth is "one of the truly few novelists
who make writing feel (ouch) like a physical function, never
mind which. Uplifting it's not, absorbing, frustrating and
alive it certainly is. "

B172   Sale, Roger.   "Enemies, Foreigners, and Friends, "
        Hudson Review, 25, 4 (1972-73), 701-14.

Barth manages to make the most--in terms of
pleasure and meaning--of the patterns of narrative art.   His
subject, turning forty and seeking rejuvenation through wom-
en, "probably would find its best form in the dirty limerick
or the shaggy dog story, " and his attitude could well be
called male chauvinistic.   But Barth's talent redeems.
"Chimera is the best thing he's done since some early
scenes in The End of the Road. "

B173   Scholes, Robert. "The Allegory of Exhaustion," Fiction International, 1 (fall 1973), 106-08.

Chimera, like Balzac's "Unknown Masterpiece" and Henry James' artist stories, belongs in the special category of "esthetic allegory." Lost in the Funhouse was "worthy of comparison with James." From such a comparison, we derive the realization that for James, writing at the height of the Religion of Art, "the satisfactions of art are sufficient compensation for the sacrifices," while for Barth, writing today, "being an artist is only a poor substitute for being a lover." Chimera makes the reader aware that "we live in a heritage of mythic patterns which shape our lives in ineluctable ways. There are mythic messages in the genes of people as well as in the formulaic necessities of fiction." The effect of becoming aware of this situation is crippling. "Critical knowledge has got to the point where it is paralysing the arts. Everybody knows too much for great art to be produced in any established form. And those most likely to produce it know best and suffer most from the knowledge."

B174   Sheppard, R. Z. "Scheherazade and Friends," Time, 100, 14 (October 2, 1972), 80.

From the first to the most recent, "there is no real urgency in Barth's novels. His characters exhibit a comfortable, charming nihilism." The two later tales of Chimera falter, but "Dunyazadiad" is successful and strong. Art and love, "which become pretty much the same thing before Barth gets through " are "among the few things that Barth seems to take very seriously."

B175   Shrapnel, Norman. "Myth-Making with a Rib-Tickler," The Guardian, 111, 4 (July 26, 1974), 21.

Those who take a reverential approach to myth will be disconcerted and perhaps angered by Barth's "rib-tickling techniques," "joky intellectualism," and "common-room nudges." Others, however, will be delighted by his wit, imaginative vigor, and skill.

B176   Wood, Michael. "New Fall Fiction," New York Review of Books, 19, 6 (October 19, 1972), 33-37.

Chimera is troubled by "a thorough deadness of language, which belies all the book's apparent mental activity, makes it seem a fraud. Barth seems to have something like an unwillingness to <u>write</u>, as distinct from simply publishing." Barth's mind, as it can be perceived through his prose, is more interesting than his books.   He cheapens his own intelligence through a kind of aristocratic disdain which expresses itself in a refusal to do more than <u>play</u> with language.   "He is a narrative chauvinistic pig."

ARTICLES

C1   Bean, John C.   "John Barth and Festive Comedy: The
      Failure of Imagination in The Sot-Weed Factor,"
      Xavier University Studies, 10, 1 (1971), 3-15.

        "The recent trend toward fantasy novels--in writers
as diverse as Barth, Pynchon, Hawkes, Vonnegut, Tolkien--
suggests that one result of the post-existential mood is a
wide, new demand on imagination itself." In "The Literature
of Exhaustion," Barth has explicitly proposed the redemptive
and regenerative value of inventiveness. This is the orientation of the festive comedies of such writers as Shakespeare,
Cervantes, and Fielding. The Sot-Weed Factor follows the
structural conventions of festive comedy, but its world-view,
being existentially pessimistic, is completely antithetical to
the mode. Barth's characters dread experience and change;
they move toward dissipation rather than renewal. The order artificially imposed by the author does not, as in true
festive comedy, magically transform the world for the bet-
ter. Barth's artificiality makes us aware only of his own
juggler-like manipulations. His is an imaginativeness that
fails to redeem. "The literature of exhaustion becomes itself exhausted."

C2   Bienstock, Beverly Gray.   "Lingering on the Autognos-
      tic Verge: John Barth's Lost in the Funhouse,"
      Modern Fiction Studies, 19, 1 (1973), 69-78.

        All the stories of Lost in the Funhouse "revolve
around the search for one's identity amidst the tangled skeins
of past, present, and future." Barth sees an "eternal re-
currence," involving both progress and simultaneity, opera-
tive in his universe. Proteus, who has "exhausted the guises
of reality," represents Barth's fascination with "exhausted
possibility." Only works of art partake of a "capricious im-
mortality." Artist, work of art, and reader merge in a
continuous cycle. Identity is never fixed. "We go on for-

48

ever exchanging masks in a fantastic hall of mirrors, and
one shouldn't try to tell the dancer from the dance."

C3   Binni, Francesco. "John Barth e il romanzo di so-
cietà," Studi Americani, 12 (1966), 277-300.

C4   Bluestone, George. "John Wain and John Barth: The
Angry and the Accurate," Massachusetts Review, 1,
3 (1960), 582-89.

Despite his comparative lack of publicity, John Barth
is a more effective and more authentically unorthodox novelist than John Wain. The Floating Opera is "a Rabelaisian
farce" about "a sort of buccaneer lawyer on the Eastern
Shore of Maryland" who learns that there is no more reason
to die than to stay alive. A letter from Barth indicates that
The End of The Road is intended as a scuttling of Todd Andrews' findings: " 'I deliberately had him end up with that
brave ethical subjectivism in order that Jacob Horner might un-
do that position in #2 and carry all non-mystical value-thinking to the end of the road.' " The abortion scene illustrates
the cost of placing "glib articulation before instinctive humanity." Barth is willing to face the fact that "we must some-
how allow for what reason and language cannot contain." His
work may mark the emergence of a new genre--"the serious
farce."

C5   Bradbury, John M. "Absurd Insurrection: The Barth-
Percy Affair," South Atlantic Quarterly, 18, 3 (1969),
319-29.

John Barth and Walker Percy represent a new phase
in the Southern Renaissance. "It is patently futile, even im-
pertinent, to seek answers or cures in Barth's work. He is
essentially a fabulist, and a prodigious one at that, achieving
his effects like a Swift or a Sterne largely through irony and
parody. His unifying subject may be value-thinking or innocence or history in the remaking, but as an artist his end is
'Articulation!' "

C6   Brooks, Peter. "John Barth," Encounter, 28, 6 (1967),
71-75.

Barth delights in triangular mirror relationships, unreliable narration, and fabulation. "Structure and script indeed exist, like all Barthian systems, for their internal contradictions are even more fun than systems." His aspiration

towards the state of moral allegory" gives an inappropriate
ending to The End of The Road. When combined with the
"insinuation of a 20th century consciousness" into the historical realm, it renders The Sot-Weed Factor, for all its bril-
liance and sweep, an ultimately boring pursuit of Significance.
Giles Goat-Boy is "a conte moral raised to the epic dimension." The blatantness of the controlling analogue effectively turns our attention from exegesis to the larger intellectual
framework in which contemporary political and social issues
have their being. The book makes large claims and is in
fact a continual intellectual challenge, but it has a flaw that
is unsettling. "The rhetoric of affection, acceptance, and
embrace which we get at the end seems to me to fail (quite
in the manner of End of the Road) because its language vio-
lates the critical intelligence to which the novel has trained
us."

C7   Davis, Cynthia. " 'The Key to the Treasure': Narra-
       tive Movements and Effects in Chimera," Journal of
       Narrative Technique, 5, 2 (1975), 105-15.

       The "Dunyazadiad" is composed of seven concentric
narrative frames which represent "the interaction between the
artist and his tradition." The spiral-image is appropriate to
the book as a whole because each of the novellas is "a kind
of commentary on the other two, and their order represents
a gradual extension and investigation of narrative techniques
as well as thematic concerns." The "reverse-frame" technique is particularly effective in conveying Barth's realization
that a reciprocal balance must be attained between the individual artist and tradition, reality and artifice, and purely
aesthetic patternings and prosaic issues.

C8   Dippie, Brian W. " 'His Visage Wild; His Form Ex-
       otick': Indian Themes and Cultural Guilt in John
       Barth's The Sot-Weed Factor," American Quarterly,
       21, 1 (1969), 113-121.

       The Sot-Weed Factor is "an exposé of certain favor-
ite American myths" which reveals the white cultural guilt in
regard to Indians and Negroes that "made from the outset the
dream of Eden and Adam a vast, ironic joke." The white
America that Eben comes to is not a land of promise and innocence, but a hotbed of rampant corruption. His progression from innocence to disillusionment to self-sufficiency parallels Candide's. The threatened rebellion by Indians and Negroes embodies a terror which, as D. H. Lawrence and Les-

lie Fiedler have pointed out, is latent in the American
psyche. Eben's brotherhood with Quassapelagh and Drepacca
is a realization through mutual decency of the dream whose
lustful version Barth rejects in his lampooning of the Pocahontas-John Smith legend. Burlingame's search for progeni-
tors and the Billy Rumbly episode suggest "an inborn, ir-
revocable antipathy between white and Indian." Though Eben
is not a typical American figure, his experiences do stress
the "spiritual sterility of the New World" and establish him
as "a kind of frontier pragmatist, stripped of all preconceptions and illusions by the environment."

C9   Diser, Philip E.   "The Historical Ebenezer Cooke,"
        Critique, 10, 3 (1968), 48-59.

        "An Ebenezer Cooke wrote a poem entitled The Sot-
Weed Factor, and it is not accurate to suggest that the name
is a pseudonym or that nothing is known of his life." Barth
employs most of the circumstantial evidence available in his
novel, and, moreover, he "is familiar with and quotes from
Cooke's original poem." A point-by-point comparison of the
two works reveals that Barth has used the original poem "as
a general guide to some of the experiences of the fictional
Ebenezer in Maryland and to some topical details to make his
minor action historically accurate." Part of the delight of
Barth's novel is that it "mocks those historical novels and
biographies that build elaborate books around similarly
skimpy factual information."

C10   Ewell, Barbara. "John Barth: The Artist of History,"
        Southern Literary Journal, 5, 2 (1973), 32-46.

        The contrast between Burlingame, who comes to
grips with his present and his future only through the embracing of a particular past, and Eben, who finds the past
unamenable to his overly simplistic reductions, is an expression of Barth's ambivalence in regard to the issue of pattern
and flux. Only through the enlightened assertion of identity
and values is a resolution possible--a resolution which entails acknowledging all the necessary qualifications while affirming that imposed order, once accepted, is the only basis
for history, art, culture, or ethics.

C11   "Existential Comedian," Time, 89, 11 (March 17,
        1967), 109.

        Barth knows better than to take anything, including

himself, too seriously. His characters "are never cast as
heroes: there is something slightly ludicrous about them
all." His four novels--which have sold a grand total of
58,000 copies (50,000 for Giles Goat-Boy, 8,000 for the other three combined)--"trace the systematic progress of the
anti-novelist." After the apprentice work of The Floating
Opera and The End of the Road, "Barth abandoned all allegi-
ance to the novel's disciplines; he set out to exploit the
form's deficiencies by overdoing them."

C12   Garis, Robert. "What Happened to John Barth?" Com-
        mentary, 42, 4 (1966), 189-95. [See items B77
        B83, B95, B114, B116.]

        In The Sot-Weed Factor and Giles Goat-Boy, Barth
undertakes "the resurrection of the pre-dramatic novel"--a
task entailing a necessary and perhaps deliberate tediousness.
The episodic structure of these two works "has the effect of
casting a merciless spotlight on the puerility of [Barth's]
thinking." The books offer only a "few sophomoric para-
doxes." The Sot-Weed Factor evidences "Barth's sheer in-
capacity to invent interesting episodes or interesting language." Giles Goat-Boy fails to live up to the Swiftian allegory it emulates. "We learn nothing new about the way our
world works simply by having it called a university; Barth,
in fact, hardly ever describes the world in terms of a university, and even when he does, there is no meaningful
counterpart in our world to what happens in Barth's university. It's all on the surface, all a matter of substituting
one term for another." One of the major aspects of Barth's
originality is "his continual preoccupation with basic, almost
naive, moral and ethical questions." The End of the Road
is a superior novel because in it "Barth 'thinks through' such
questions in the way most good fiction characteristically op-
erates--by dramatizing them in terms of complex, convincing-
ly rendered personal relations; and he 'answers' them by con-
triving a satisfying outcome to the drama of these relations."
Perhaps because Barth has been influenced by "fashionable
modern literary criticism" to abandon the more realistic techniques at which he excels, "he is no longer writing about
identity-crises but going through one himself, and in public."
He lacks "the special verbal gifts of a Nabokov" essential to
the methods he now regrettably aspires to employ.

C13   Graff, Gerald. "Mythotherapy and Modern Poetics,"
        Triquarterly, 11 (1968), 76-90.

Jacob Horner suffers paralysis as a result of his inability to choose among "the infinite number of possible hypotheses concerning the events of his life." Joe Morgan believes that action can be based upon a set of personal subjective values so long as one remains consistently faithful to those arbitrary preferences. But he fails by his own standard. His fundamental mistake is to assume that the self is singular and knowable. Mythotherapy, on the other hand, implies that "roles and fictions have no corresponding essence in the object." Causal relationships are non-existent; experience is fragmentary and disjunctive. "Reality is radically incommensurable with all ideas and judgments about it," and consequently the self is "locked within a prison of its subjective myths from which there can be no possible escape."

C14   Gross, Beverly.   "The Anti-Novels of John Barth,"
      Chicago Review, 20, 3 (1968), 95-109.

Barth's fiction has been moving toward "the repudiation of narrative art." Nihilism, which was merely a "quirk of character" and a "device" in The Floating Opera and The End of the Road, has become the thematic and formalistic end product of The Sot-Weed Factor and Giles Goat-Boy. Barth's gamesmanship pervades all the works and grows increasingly desperate. The tangled relationships of The Floating Opera demonstrate "the impossible strain of human attachment and commitment." A "desperately sick" Jacob Horner lures the reader into an ironic, black humorist attitude toward emotions in The End of the Road, only to have that perspective undercut by the irreducible horror of Rennie's death. Ebenezer Cooke and George Giles begin as bumpkins and end as "vehicles for despair"--Eben because he learns that "there are no ends in life," George because he learns that "there are no Answers." The formal aspects of the books reflect these contentions: the myriad plot complexities of The Sot-Weed Factor, subject to insufficient and chance resolutions, are an embodiment of futility; Giles Goat-Boy is "a dialectic without a synthesis." Thus each book becomes "an anti-novelistic assault on itself." Each is a role for John Barth who is seeking his own identity. As such, none is adequate. Yet, despite the dubiety expressed in every work from The Floating Opera to "Title," fiction remains a necessary and mildly affirmative endeavor for Barth. "He is not quite affirming life but he is negating lifelessness. He is not quite affirming art but he is negating silence."

C15   Hendin, Josephine.   "John Barth's Fictions for Survival,"

Harper's Magazine, 247, 1480 (September 1973), 102-06.

All of Barth's works imply that personal identity and private emotion are painful, unsatisfying, and futile. Each of his principal characters seeks a means of escape from self-- through detachment, through multiplicity, but above all through intense verbal artistry. "For Barth's people, style is life-style, the logic of sentences refutes the mind's chaos, syntax can be a saving grace and parody the only force for order." They are redeemed by their ability, in life and in art, to practice a willing suspension of disbelief. "Magic words are all in all; storytelling is life's means and only prize."

C16 Hinden, Michael. "Lost in the Funhouse: Barth's Use of the Recent Past," Twentieth Century Literature, 19, 2 (1973), 107-18.

"Joycean patterns dominate Lost in the Funhouse and may be found in the determinative structural elements as well as in minute intricacies of style." But the book goes beyond parody to embody Barth's concept of the Baroque by "defining and exhausting its own possibilities." The particular sequence of the pieces suggests "an aesthetic circularity" which reinforces the theme. The first seven stories stress "the problems of his art." "Menelaiad" and "Anonymiad" are "the true masterpieces" of the volume. Faced with Camus's absurd, Menelaus finds that he is able to "multiply what he cannot unify." Barth advocates cutting loose from the recent past, but, at the same time, he employs the materials of that past for new art, thereby executing "a Prodigal Son's circuitous return."

C17 Hirsch, David. "John Barth's Freedom Road," Mediterranean Review, 2, 3 (1972), 38-47.

The End of the Road is a novel about the search for identity in which the protagonist discovers that "the self does not exist, or that if it exists it exists as a necessary fiction." (The history of the theme of self-knowledge is discussed with reference to Oedipus, Abraham, Descartes, Erich Fromm, Camus, Poe, Dostoevsky, Melville, Berkeley, Socrates, and Leon Shestov.) The Remobilization Farm is a metaphor for the world, the Progress and Advice Room for the absurdity of man's condition. Barth's view denies the possibility of real freedom and shatters the concept of self

which "was once thought the basic unit of human existence."
For Jake, consciousness leads to the negation of personal
existence and the dubiety of external objectivity. The ego,
as mask, is simply a partition between two voids, one internal and one external. "It is only after life has been
molded into a recognizable shape through art that it begins
to radiate meaning." But the Knowledge and Imagination
which are associated with form are for Jake, as they are in
Genesis, stultifying and pernicious. The indeterminacy of
his character is Jake's rebellious response, his attempt to
go beyond values and form. Thus freed from divine authori-
tarianism but caught in "the vegetable pattern of meaningless
growth and decay," man is "tossed between the Scylla and
Charybdis of meaningless freedom and strangulating form."
Barth's subsequent fiction evinces a move away from "relatively well ordered structures" toward "new modes of sensibility in which form has become subordinate to the artist's
freedom to invent worlds of his own."

C18 Holder, Alan. " 'What Marvelous Plot ... Was
     Afoot?': History in Barth's The Sot-Weed Factor,"
     American Quarterly, 20, 3 (1968), 596-604.

     The Sot-Weed Factor is informed by an impulse to
"debunk the past," particularly by portraying colonial history
as a web of selfish and energetic plots. In developing this
concept of "history as intrigue," Barth alters and adds to the
accounts actually found in the Archives of Maryland, with the
result that "one is not sure whether he is seriously offering
the various plots as his conception of the actual shape of
events, or whether he is simply indulging a storyteller's desire to tidy up the clutter of history and mold it into a narrative pattern." Barth seems determined to play with history. Like Eben, the author has expressed a temperamental
imperviousness to factuality. His novel gives implicit ap-
probation to those characters who, in contrast to the latent
cosmopsis of Eben, persist in willful action, by toying with
governments the way Barth toys with facts. Burlingame is
dialectically torn between the philosophic freedom of being
an orphan and Cosmic Lover standing outside Nature, and his
desire to find a link with the past and a father, which would
enable him to "discover moral boundaries and limits of identity." The Sot-Weed Factor, which "refuses to commit itself to a particular conception of the past, of historical truth,
but wants the freedom to embrace simultaneously a variety of
possibilities," stands in the relation of a Cosmic Lover to
the past. Its ideas, "even when offered in seriousness, may

be said to be inadequately felt." The impression it leaves is not of a work molded by an historical imperative, but of "an abstract exercise in form."

C19   Jones, D. Allan. "The Game of the Name in Barth's The Sot-Weed Factor," Research Studies (Washington State University, Pullman), 40, 3 (1972), 219-21.

The many possible components and derivatives of the name Henry Burlingame III--"burl," "burling," "game," "Henry," "III," "burly," "burley"--directly reflect that character's role(s) in the novel.

C20   Kennard, Jean E. "John Barth: Imitations of Imitations," Mosaic, 3, 2 (1970), 116-31.

"The direct influence of Existential ideas upon the work of John Barth is probably more clearly marked than upon that of any other contemporary American novelist." These ideas have influenced particularly the form of The Sot-Weed Factor and Giles Goat-Boy. An imitation of an imitation comes into being when one parodies, through exaggeration, a work of art which is itself by definition an imitation of life; when one ironically transposes a particular work from one era to another; or when one creates a series of concentric authors. In The Sot-Weed Factor multiple character guises are used to deny absolute personality and, by continually foiling reader expectations, to bring the reader repeatedly to the Pit, "that mental state of absolute confusion in which all points of certainty are removed." Giles Goat-Boy is an imitation by virtue of serial deception. "Everything it states is shown to be an illusion by everything that follows." The author, moreover, is consciously playing the role of the author. The allegory effectively illustrates "the inadequacy of all ways of approaching the world." Thus the book supports "the Existential premise that everything is ultimately subjective."

C21   Kiely, Benedict. "Ripeness Was Not All: John Barth's Giles Goat-Boy," Hollins Critic, 3 (December 1966), 1-12; reprinted and expanded in R. H. W. Dillard, George Garrett and John Rees Moore, eds., The Sounder Few (Athens: University of Georgia Press, 1971), 195-210.

A highly appreciative and highly impressionistic survey of the body of Barth's work. Rather than presenting a structured argument, the article imaginatively combines di-

verse Barthian themes, images, characters, precursors, allusions, and plots in dashing and highly compressed language.
It is, therefore, virtually impossible to summarize. Consider a typical sentence: "Ebenezer is the poet, as Billy Bocks-
fuss or Giles Goat-Boy is hero and prophet and messiah, the
poet, let me say, lost stumbling and astray in an unkind
world where men may steal the Kingdom into which he ex-
pects to come and make of it a den of thieves and harlots
and may steal even his title to poetry, his identity."

C22   Kiernan, Robert F.   "John Barth's Artist in the Fun
      House," Studies in Short Fiction, 10, 4 (1973), 273-
      80.

Lost in the Funhouse approaches the form of a
Künstlerroman.   The three Ambrose stories "trace the growth
of a vocation to art."   The fact that the mode of narration
becomes more verbally sophisticated as Ambrose matures and
becomes self-consciously fascinated with language indicates
that the teller and subject are one.   "Night-Sea Journey"
"dramatizes the prenatal period of Ambrose's life."   "Autobiography" demonstrates that "fiction tends necessarily to a
life of its own and to an inordinate degree of self-reflection."
"Petition" is probably "a projection of Ambrose's rivalry with
his brother into an imaginative and very literary fiction."
"Echo" develops "a fiction emblematic of the ambiguities of
narration in the first six stories of the sequence" and marks
the transition of Ambrose from explicit to implicit subject.
"Two Meditations" is "the key to understanding all of the subsequent stories" because it is the first in which the author
attains his goal of eradicating his own excessive presence.
"Title," on the other hand, utilizes a contrary stratagem--
"an attempt to implement as much self-consciousness as possible and to expel self-consciousness by an inundation of consciousness."   The attempt fails.   The "formal gimmickery"
of "Glossolalia" betrays "the continuing need of Ambrose to
escape from himself in his fictions."   "Life-Story" finds both
narrator and author pulled into the fiction and constitutes the
last effort of the narrator to efface himself through "ingeni-
ous and esoteric strategies."   In "Menelaiad," Ambrose attempts a more conventional tack--"an Homeric-Conradian effort to obscure authorial presence by an intricate nest of
speakers, modulated by an overtone of Joycean myth-ground-
ing"--but produces only "intolerably subjective gimmickery."
The speaker of "Anonymiad," a "composite Ambrose," returns to a primal form of narrative and "simply refuses to
become embroiled in the problems that are the subject of the
sequence."

C23   Knapp, Edgar H.   "Found in the Barthhouse: Novelist
      as Savior," Modern Fiction Studies, 14, 4 (1968-69),
      446-51.

      Lost in the Funhouse "adheres to the archetypal pat-
tern of passage through difficult ways," and is a "mixture of
myth, masque, cinema, and symposium."   The tidewater setting functions mythically as "an ironic garden" where Ambrose
experiences "heroic suffering, death, and resurrection."   The
six characters enact "a masque-like drama symbolic of the
inner transactions which result in human behavior," oscilla-
tion between members of the same generations creating "syn-
chronic resonance," while that between members of different
generations creates "diachronic resonance."   Cinematic splic-
ing of scenes, synthesis of fantasy and action, freezes, juxta-
positions of sound and image, allegorical blocking of scenes
into "symbolic ballet," and sensory imagery all contribute to
"the basic theme of the merging of illusion and reality."
Point of view in the story is composed of "six distinct bands
of mental formulation" which fall into two camps--that of
"narrative" and that of "conscience"--between which a running dialogue, or symposium, is sustained.   Thus the reader
is continually reminded of "the contrivance of literature,"
and of the fact that literature, like human families, is subject to generational modification of the same archetypal form.

C24   Kyle, Carol A.   "The Unity of Anatomy: The Structure
      of Barth's Lost in the Funhouse," Critique, 13, 3
      (1972), 31-43.

      Because of the work's diversity, "only Frye's defi-
nition of anatomy could ever justify the structural unity of
Barth's most recent prose fiction."   Frye's concept is that
of "a work whose unity is an intellectual concept so lively
that it can spin out of its own energy a self-contained, fanci-
ful, and witty anti-novel," a work which employs multiple
voices, freely associative conversation parodying standard
prose fiction, and unorthodox conventions of time and physical proportions.   Lost in the Funhouse is thus comparable
to Tristram Shandy, Orlando, The Anatomy of Melancholy and
Steppenwolf.   It is also "a microcosmic anatomy of criticism," which plays off of two major fictional forms, "the
absurd and the autobiographical."   Among the themes turned
up in a systematic survey of the stories are: perpetual
journeying, the equating of identity with speech, adolescent
initiation, love and sex, artistic detachment, madness, parodic treatment of myth and literary convention, and the in-

separability of "words from speaker, medium from message, and dancer from dance."

C25   LeClair, Thomas. "Death and Black Humor," Critique, 17, 1 (1975), 5-40 [especially 17-19, 35].

When faced with the prospect of death, "the hero-narrators of The Floating Opera and [John Hawkes'] Second Skin expand and refine the strategy of deception to, literally, an art. They make their narrations life 'stories,' elaborate fictions which conceal or deny the degree to which death has dictated their lives." Contradictions and inconsistencies prove Todd to be an unreliable narrator. His rationale involves "ultimate irresponsibility to fact, irrelevance of contradiction, formal integrity, and life as a fiction to be given an aesthetic order." Unable to cope otherwise with the knowledge of his own physical mortality, "Todd invents fictional selves and roles to substitute for himself." He is the first of a series of "protean fictionalizers" with whom Barth identifies. "Barth finds man a pretentious fool, a being whose finest power--the mind--can do little to mediate the fact that it will be extinguished. Only the solipsistic imagination can both protect and make interesting a life whose temporality and physicality are a burden."

C26   _____. "John Barth's The Floating Opera: Death and the Craft of Fiction," Texas Studies in Language and Literature, 14, 4 (1973), 711-30.

Barth's narrators are "protean fictionalizers" who are by definition unreliable. "Unable or unwilling to establish a continuity of emotional engagement with experience--especially, in the early work, with the unthinkable final fact of death, an impossible necessity--these men imaginatively distort their experience into manageable shapes by creating life 'stories.'" Todd Andrews contradicts himself both in his philosophical generalizations and in the contrast between his espoused convictions and his acts. Factual unreliability is endemic to Todd's aesthetic which, like his practice of law, is predicated upon personal irresponsibility. His boats symbolize "Todd's willful avoidance of fact or reality"--a proclivity for which The Floating Opera is the synthetic metaphor. The work's nihilism is "epistemological first, valuative second." The Doctor in The End of the Road extends the aesthetic of Todd and Barth. Those who rely upon limited reason are doomed. Burlingame is Barth's representative in The Sot-Weed Factor, as is Harold Bray in Giles Goat-Boy--

creators who transcend their own creations. Barth evinces a
growing tendency to lure the reader into false assumptions
with tidbits of autobiographical data. At the same time, a
burgeoning preoccupation with sexual and creative impotence
is seen, particularly in Lost in the Funhouse. But these elements must be understood as the devices of man "who is
sure that all constructs, including sincerity, are illusive."

C27 Lee, L. L. "Some Uses of Finnegans Wake in John
      Barth's The Sot-Weed Factor, James Joyce Quarter-
      ly, 5, 2 (1968), 177-78.

      When Burlingame explains his disguise as Nicholas
Lowe to Eben, he uses the sentence, "Thus was Nicky Lowe
born, ex nihilo and without travail!" This is obviously a re-
working of Finnegans Wake, page 23, lines 16-17: "O foenix
culprit! Ex nickylow malo comes mickelmassed bonum."
We should observe that "Joyce's sentences are essential to
Barth's novel, reinforcing the themes and attitudes of that
work: innocence, original sin, and the ambiguity and multi-
fariousness of the world." The Sot-Weed Factor chapter
that follows the sentence quoted above, a discourse called "A
Layman's Pandect (ALP), on twinship," constitutes another
obvious parallel. "If HCE has twin sons and is everybody,
Burlingame, who is Nicky Lowe but also, surely, mickelmassed bonum, loves everybody, the cosmos. Not only that,
he jollily accuses Ebenezer and Anna of an unconscious in-
cestuous love. EC and Anna are, in more ways than one,
shapes of HCE and ALP.... In short, [Finnegans Wake] is
one or both parents of [The Sot-Weed Factor]."

C28 McDonald, James L. "Barth's Syllabus: The Frame
      of Giles Goat-Boy," Critique, 13, 3 (1972), 5-10.

      There are two sacred books in Giles Goat-Boy, one
within the other: the R. N. S. prepared by Giles(,) Stoker,
and Giles Goat-Boy; or, The Revised New Syllabus by John
Barth which envelopes it. The frame which differentiates
these two is composed of the various disclaimers, editors'
comments, cover letter, and postscript material. This
frame is "both functional and necessary" because, by calling
attention to the artificiality of the document at hand, it en-
forces the major implications of the work as a whole: that
not the reliability of authorship nor the consensus of critical
opinion, but "the glaring authenticity of the narrative itself"
establishes its truth; that, as a "Syllabus," the book presents
not a firm didactic moral but "a tentative outline or lesson

plan, which is subject to change"; and that, "as fiction, artifact, constructed absolute," it offers a coherent alternative
to the flux of the modern world.

C29   Majdiak, Daniel. "Barth and the Representation of
      Life," Criticism, 12, 1 (1970), 51-67.

      Both the theme and technique of The End of the Road
may profitably be studied in terms of the perspective raised
by "The Literature of Exhaustion." As is evident from its
opening sentence, the novel concerns the problem of multiplicity of personal identity. Between them, Joe Morgan and
Jacob Horner create a complete picture of Barthian nihilism.
"Morgan represents the older form which, setting itself in
opposition to the transcendental, attempts to establish value
in the rational will. He is destroyed because he does not
see that man is ruled by other human factors. The new ni-
hilists like Horner attempt to take these factors into account
and their stance is that moral codes are nothing but matters
of feeling or social pressure. But Horner is destroyed by
Cosmopsis, the vision that begins with ironical detachment
but ends in sheer bafflement." Barth uses parody to rein-
force the theme of nihilism by "forcing the characters to
realize their unreality." This tactic involves such devices as
indeterminate identity, vitalization of a stock character, arti-
ficialization of setting, environmental parallelisms, violation
of ordinary time progression, reduction of characters at
critical moments, and self-avowed editing by the narration.
Their purpose is to emphasize rather than minimize "the
unreality of literature" in an effort to "discredit the norms
which the novel assumes" and produce "a more credible picture of reality through a more viable fictional form." Within the novel, the difference is represented by the contrast
between Scriptotherapy and Mythotherapy. Scriptotherapy is
based on the realization that "to talk about experience in order to create a self is to transform it into fiction." It is
therefore superior. "While Mythotherapy deals with people
and attempts to control lives, Scriptotherapy deals solely
with form, with fiction. But in its self-conscious use of
fiction it exposes our fantasies and reminds us of our pro-
pensity to regard them as reality, whereas Mythotherapy can
only serve to enforce them."

C30   Mercer, Peter. "The Rhetoric of Giles Goat-Boy,"
      Novel: A Forum on Fiction, 4, 2 (1971), 147-58.

      The rhetoric of Giles Goat-Boy functions as a central

"formative element" of the work in a number of important
ways. The distinctive qualities of the narrator's wide-rang-
ing style "provide linguistic proof of the uniqueness of Giles"
and lends credibility to his claims of election. It is composed of four intermingling tendencies--the heroic and comic
"styles" and the academic and goatish "registers"--all marked
by strong rhythm, Latinate locutions, archaic and idiosyn-
cratic diction. The clash of these two language sets parallels the thematic allegorical tension between the animal and
intellectual poles of human nature, and generates a comic
contrast between high manner and vulgar material. It thereby embodies, from the beginning, the synthesizing impulse
which informs the entire work. The "robust, tragi-comic
inclusiveness" of the language conditions our response to the
three phases of Giles' quest. In the first, which depends
upon adamant differentiation, we "naturally resist Giles' fa-
natical attempt to exclude and deny kinds of experience that
the rhetoric has happily, not to say exuberantly accommo-
dated." In the second, which is the opposite of the first,
"we miss the complexity and intellectual richness ... that we
perceived in the earlier rhetoric." But in the third, "the
components of the rhetoric tend to merge with each other and
the gap between Giles and the rhetoric closes." The comic
devices of the Revised New Syllabus can be attributed to
Giles', and Barth's, "acute consciousness of the dangers of
posturing and of solemnity" in a skeptical age. The devices
can be dropped in the Posttape becaue it is purportedly a
private rather than a public recitation, but distancing is
maintained by the suggestion of spuriousness.

C31 Miller, Russell H. "The Sot-Weed Factor: A Con-
     temporary Mock-Epic," Critique, 8, 2 (1965-66),
     88-100.

"Although the metaphysics of Barth's novel may be
modern and perhaps even original, the structure is traditional. The vehicle which Barth has chosen is the mock-epic
genre, a genre which has traditionally allowed for mixture of
the comic and the profound." Like the productions of Pope
and Dryden, this is "an essentially comic work which makes
an essentially serious statement about man and society."
Barth establishes his genre through a great number of devices: allusions to other epic and mock-epic works; comments on epic theory; the identification of Eben as an Odys-
seus-figure and repeated parallelism with The Odyssey; comic disparity between elevated diction and its low subjects;
and comic versions of the arming of the knight, epic strug-

gles, dreams and mythological references, real history, epic
catalogues, and the courageous and mobile hero. "Eben's
eventual realization of heroism is similar, not only to Don
Quixote's, but also to the progress of another essentially
comic hero--the hero of a 'serio-comic epic poem in prose'
by Fielding, Tom Jones." Barth and others are just now
rediscovering the effectiveness of a major 18th-century mode.

C32 Morrell, David. "Ebenezer Cooke, Sot-Weed Factor
     Redivivus: The Genesis of John Barth's The Sot-
     Weed Factor," Bulletin of the Midwest Modern Lan-
     guage Association, 8, 1 (1975), 32-47.

     Barth used an informing principle in The Sot-Weed
Factor similar in its structural effect to that, derived from
Raglan and Campbell, which shapes Giles Goat-Boy. In writing his first two relatively realistic novels, Barth's ideas
about the nature of fiction changed significantly. Realism
revealed itself as both "a hamper to his imagination" and
"philosophically untenable." Since one can write only words,
and words are always necessarily a simplification and distortion of experience, the proper subject for imitation is "not
Reality itself but what we make--or what other people have
made--of Reality." Barth combined genuine (though ambiguous) 17th-century historical material with genuine (though
ironic) 18th-century literary conventions to produce a work
which espouses the fluidity of existence while imitating the
orderliness we nevertheless mentally impose upon it. Barth's
life of Ebenezer Cooke is substantially consistent both with
Lawrence Wroth's original speculative biography (1934) and
Philip Diser's subsequent schematic summary of the few docu-
mented facts (1968). But more importantly, his numerous
and obvious interpolations--often at odds with both the spirit
and the details of the poem and accepted historical accounts
(e. g., Captain Smith's adventure with Pocahontas)--imply
that, for Barth, history too is a fabric of words, and therefore a distortion, a fiction.

C33 Morris, Christopher D. "Barth and Lacan: The World
     of the Moebius Strip," Critique, 17, 1 (1975), 69-77.

     A highly technical linguistic-psychoanalytic examina-
tion of Lost in the Funhouse suggests that "the earlier critical frame may now be inadequate, and that the truly disturbing quality of the more recent work is the result of Barth's
rejection of any phenomenological self-consciousness as the
agency which vitiates nature and art. Selfhood in Lost in the

Funhouse is altogether ignored, except as a farcical or sentimental entity, and the locus of the 'narrative' affliction is
ultimately reduced to the purely linguistic problem of substi-
tution. The situation is more disturbing than the early existentialist dilemmas because the Cartesian subject has been replaced as its center by meaningless, autonomous phonemes. "

C34 Noland, Richard W. "John Barth and the Novel of
       Comic Nihilism," Wisconsin Studies in Contemporary
       Literature, 7 (1966), 239-57.

       Barth is one of those who, in the aftermath of the
death of God announced by Nietzsche, "have simply taken the
fact of nihilism as the subject matter of their work without
necessarily developing a single philosophical position on which
to base a system of values. " Todd's masks are "at least as
much an effort to avoid life as to master death. " Similarly,
the Macks "live by theory, not genuine feeling. " Barth's triangular relationships bespeak "an implicit homosexual theme,"
running through all three novels and becoming explicit in The
Sot-Weed Factor, which suggests that "society is bound together by the erotic. " Thus the failure of "this basic human
group" is "symbolic of a failure of contact of the members
of a whole society on the most basic level possible. " Todd
is a man "in whom reason and emotion run in separate direc-
tions. " He can "find value and affirm life only by a unity of
reason and emotion. " The episode of Jeannine's sickness,
despite its sentimentality, provides such an occasion. In The
End of the Road, Jake resorts to evasion and role playing,
Joe to dogmatism. Both are abstract systems and neither is
adequate to "a concrete situation in which concern and responsibility are required. " The Sot-Weed Factor presents
Eben as an American Adam and exploits many traditional
themes of American literature within the context of a modern,
existentially absurd universe. Burlingame's experience "portrays the loss of an impossible freedom, as Eben's education
portrays the loss of an impossible and dangerous innocence. "
Barth's ironic tone, his use of parody and burlesque, are the
formal correlatives of his vision. He utilizes a form which
unites the comic and tragic, and "achieves meaning through
incident rather than depth of characterization. " He has demonstrated the inadequacy of many of Western man's attempts
to establish value, but he has offered nothing in their place.
"Barth may use parody as a way of clearing his vision, but
he can hardly rest in it if he is to develop at all. "

C35 Pinsker, Sanford. "John Barth: The Teller Who

Swallowed His Tale," Studies in the Twentieth Century, 10 (1972), 55-68.

Barth has always functioned in the area between the extremes of depleted resources on the one hand and boundless experimentation on the other. He "extends the mood" of such reflexive innovators as Gide and Proust and may in fact be "the most poetic of our novelists, the one most keenly aware that writing is a self-conscious art." Barth's strength is parody, but, in applying it to the artistic process itself, he runs the risk of producing "that dead end known as self-parody." Lost in the Funhouse is knit together by a great many internal links, but it lacks a sufficient sense of progression; it is an exercise, in the manner of Scheherazade, in "holding off death with a good story." The reflexive elements have a "paralyzing effect." The parody ultimately defeats itself. "In short, Barth is not so much the great destroyer of Modernism--exaggerating its faults through extended parody, etc.--as he is the devourer of his own Art. The principle that 'fiction must acknowledge its fictiousness and metaphoric invalidity' ... might be an intriguing thesis, even the subject of an academic symposium, but, baldly stated, it is a poor narrative line on which to hang one's story."

C36 Rodrigues, Eusebio L. "The Living Sakhyan in Barth's Giles Goat-Boy," Notes on Contemporary Literature, 2, 4 (1972), 7-8.

"In the historical context TLS [the Living Sakhyan] is the Dalai Lama who fled to India after the Chinese invasion of Tibet in 1959. In mythic terms he is not the Buddha ... but a bodhisattva, a sage whose being has achieved enlightenment but who has refused Nirvana in order to be a compassionate savior of all beings. The Footnotes to Sakhyan is a Barthian miniaturization of all Eastern scriptures with Buddhist truths predominant." The confrontation between Giles and TLS represents the confrontation of Occidental and Oriental conceptions of the hero. The truths of TLS, as relayed by the Beists, show Giles the way to Commencement Gate. Though personally freed from the illusion of self, Giles does not become a bodhisattva but remains anguished by his knowledge that Western man is bound on the wheel of samsara.

C37 Rogers, Thomas. "John Barth: A Profile," Chicago Sun Times [and other newspapers'] Book Week, August 7, 1966, p. 6.

The discrepancy between the despair and worldliness of Barth's novels and the optimism and "innocence" of his person is attributed to a sustained split between common sense and imaginative understanding. "Barth has not been corrupted by his knowledge of modern life because he has never believed in it. In fact, his novels are a deliberate defiance of what he knows."

C38   Rovit, Earl. "The Novel As Parody: John Barth," Critique, 6, 2 (1963), 77-85.

The Sot-Weed Factor is a "prolonged academic joke," exhibiting more faith in the limitations than in the possibilities of imagination. If, as Barth wrote in The Floating Opera, nothing has intrinsic value, it becomes the artist's task to generate a form consonant with his own intended meaning. The two major tendencies of modern novelists are toward subjugation either "to the externally structured universe of an Alexander Pope or to the dream-emergent rhythms of an Edgar Allan Poe." The Sot-Weed Factor is in the manner of Pope by virtue of its reliance upon parody, a mode which emphasizes control and "a single shaping design." The true parody-novel "makes parody less an instrument than an end" and works ideally through satirical exposure. But if the author lacks a positive alternative to what is parodied, his work may become merely clever and bitter. Barth uses as controlling devices "the factual history of the Palatinate of Maryland and the literary conventions of the eighteenth century novel." Both are done with scrupulous accuracy, particularly the latter, which encompasses structure, theme, and language. Through the figure of Burlingame, "reminiscent of Melville's Confidence Man," Barth grapples with the contemporary question of identity, but the work is generally overburdened with "the excessive paraphernalia of authentic antiquarianism" and fails to speak to our own situation. This is probably not the novel Barth intended to write. "Barth's conscious decision to organize his talents within the circumscribing frame of a rigorous parody leads him inevitably to surrender his own moral opportunity to create values." The book reveals itself finally as "a shallow parody, an intellectual gymnastic, a mechanical puzzle in which Barth can flex the muscles of his extraordinary dexterity."

C39   Rubin, Louis D., Jr. "Notes on the Literary Scene: Their Own Language," Harper's Magazine, 230, 1379 (April 1965), 173-75.

Barth's first two books only imperfectly indicated the
flowering that transpired in his third "extravagantly original"
novel, The Sot-Weed Factor.   The work is "a fantastic
spoof of all historical novels, an outrageous compendium of
17th-century bawdry and pornography after the manner of
Rabelais, a burlesque of colonial travel diaries, a wild re-
creation of American life, and--equally as important--a bewildering inquiry into the nature of human identity in time."

C40   Ryan, Marjorie.   "Four Contemporary Satires and the
      Problem of Norms, " Satire Newsletter, 6, 2 (1969),
      40-46.

The Floating Opera "belongs in the spectrum of contemporary satire because its positive values are emotional
rather than intellectual, and because through the highly structured pattern of events and the references to Tristam Shandy,
Barth allows Todd to reveal his essential ignorance of his
deepest impulses."   Todd steadfastly attempts to withdraw
from and intellectualize his experiences, but the most deeply
felt of those experiences--his encounter with the German
soldier, the discovery of his father's body, his daughter's
illness--resist and in fact supersede his mental categoriza-
tions.   Emotional reaction, implying subjective valuative
norms, "has as much to do with his decision to live as do
his philosophical musings."

C41   Schickel, Richard.   "The Floating Opera, " Critique, 6,
      2 (1963), 53-67.

The contemporary novel of ideas tends by and large
to be comic.   The work of Barth, Berger, Heller, Percy,
Donleavy and others very nearly constitutes a school, though
their books are generally neglected both by the public and by
academic critics, none more so than The Floating Opera.
Todd is an "archetypal figure" whose bourgeois life-style and
anxiety concerning "instant annihilation" reflect the Cold War
experience.   He is an existential protagonist who has a "rage
for classification and order, " suffers "a lack of emotional
involvement with the world in general, " and "manages to en-
compass many contradictions within himself, without con-
flict. "   His prose style, "wayward, quirky, but highly
charged, " is "an accurate expression of the man. "   A count-
erpoint relationship exists between the mundane events of
Todd's day and his internal philosophical drama.   As the day
progresses, we learn that Todd's character contains several
elements of the romantic hero, that his practice of law and

building of the second boat bespeak a "withdrawal into technical excellence," and that the Inquiry is his "one great act of faith." Barth's writing escapes the monotony of many existential works, but the ending of the book is flawed: we can accept philosophically but not psychologically "the notion that Todd Andrews would be so easily converted from death to life by a child's cry." The Floating Opera metaphor is a "rationalization" for the speculative leaps unfairly demanded of the reader by the artistic failures Barth knows to be present. Barth's "comic skills" and "manipulation of language" are excellent, however, and the book as a whole more than overcomes its own flaws.

C42 Shimura, Masao. "Barth to America Bungaku no Dento," Eigo Seinen, 117 (1971), 414-16.

C43 _____. "John Barth, The End of the Road, and the Tradition of American Fiction," Studies in English Literature (English Society of Japan), 1971, 73-87.

Although Barth is more consciously concerned with narrative technique than most other American writers, he is nevertheless firmly entrenched in his native tradition. Comparisons between The End of the Road and The Wild Palms and The Sound and the Fury indicate that, like Faulkner, Barth manifests a strong "baroque impulse" which denies contradictions. Other specific similarities to The Scarlet Letter bespeak a deep affinity between Barth and the moral allegorist Hawthorne.

C44 Slethaug, Gordon E. "Barth's Refutation of the Idea of Progress," Critique, 13, 3 (1972), 11-29.

Barth begins treating history fully in The Sot-Weed Factor, where Ebenezer Cooke's growth to maturity is portrayed as "a movement from an idealist view of life, which, in effect, is a belief in progress, to a more responsible view of life which takes into account man's innate depravity." The structure of the book, like the structure of Eben's life, implies at best a cyclic view of history. "Each person's life appears to follow a cyclical pattern, which tends to repeat itself in the lives of previous and subsequent generations." This view is expanded by George's realization of Max's Law of Cyclology in Giles Goat-Boy, with the addition of a belief in love, the great "Her," as the embodiment of the requisite balancing of polarities and source of renewal. In Lost in the Funhouse the lives of the various personae "basically retrace the development of both Ebenezer and Giles," and the question of the exhaustibility of literary forms is here tied with this historical-personal theme: "Like the lives of the heroes, literary styles tend to reiterate themselves in cyclical patterns."

C45 Smith, Herbert F. "Barth's Endless Road," Critique, 6, 2 (1963), 68-76.

"Barth's world is Einstein's world," and The End of the Road is "a constant flux of ethical and personal relations," created primarily through the devices of imperfect vision and parody. The book succeeds "not because of any realistic action described in it, but because of the non-realistic effects of a series of allegorical tableaux, representing ethical positions (not characters) in opposition." Jacob Horner's kinship with Todd Andrews is evident in their sharing of "nearly identical schizophrenic symptoms of nihilism," but Jake's vision is even more restricted than Todd's. Barth uses parody (of the stereotypic love-triangle in the Horner-Morgans relationship and of existentialism in the Doctor) as "a vade mecum from the patently ridiculous literal level of the novel to its more serious abstract ethical level." Responsibility is carefully balanced among the three members of the triangle, and the trio passes through two phases: the pre-adultery phase in which Rennie represents a tabula rasa for which Jacob and Joe, representing Satan and God, or moral nihilism and ethical positivism, contend; and the post-adultery phase in which, as in the era after the Fall, Joe becomes "a God who does not understand what has happened to his otherwise sufficient rules of causality." Joe assumed the role of God when he "raised his absolute of consistency from a personal application to an absolute of action for Jacob."

C46 Summavilla, Guido. "Il cinismo cosmico di John Barth," Letture, 24 (1969), 98-110.

C47 Stubbs, John C. "John Barth As a Novelist of Ideas: The Themes of Value and Identity," Critique, 8, 2 (1965-66), 101-16.

"Primarily, John Barth is a novelist of ideas. The situations in his comic works are always directed toward establishing his twin themes of the individual's quests for value and identity in a world of gratuitous events." The Barthian hero is made to accept and affirm an absurd world and to find relative value "in the sympathy he feels for other individuals in the same plight." So doing, "he will come to accept the limits of his own identity." Todd Andrews is an historically and metaphysically representative modern hero. Despite his preoccupation with animality and absurdity, despite his discovery that there are no absolute values and no reason to live, Todd ends by affirming his irrational nature and "the relative value of his emotions." Jacob Horner, who is "unable to choose a relative value on which to organize his life," is confronted by Joe Morgan who threatens to oversimplify his identity through advocating one role, and by the Negro doctor who threatens fragmentation through advocating a series of roles. Jake discovers that human beings are too complex for either alternative. Both Jake and Joe ought to take responsibility in regard to Rennie "for the crime of violating the uniqueness of her identity," but only Jake accepts his. In The Sot-Weed Factor, Barth makes his point through "the destruction of a false ideal of innocence." The artificiality of form allows theme to dominate action and characterization. "Ambrose His Mark" is a comparatively weak reiteration of the same themes.

C48   Sugiura, Ginsaku. "Imitations-of-Novels--John Barth no Shosetsu," Eigo Seinen (Tokyo), 115 (1969), 612-13.

C49   Tanner, Stephen L. "John Barth's Hamlet," Southwest Review, 56, 4 (1971), 347-54.

As suggested by a number of allusions and situational parallels, Todd Andrews, "the prototypic rational man," is "a kind of twentieth-century Hamlet"--that is, "a 'cerebral' character who finds himself in an irrational world." He reacts by adopting an absurdist philosophy and by opting for "the 'not to be' alternative." The foiling of his suicide attempt precipitates a new frame of mind, a new possibility. "The reason that Todd was so affected by his concern for Jeannine is that for the first time he had experienced a positive emotion, love: this jarred his conclusions and caused him to reexamine his philosophy." This is an irrational positive reaction which throws into disadvantaged contrast Todd's former hyperrationalism. Hamlet's question, and all the figures in the novel associated with it (Todd, Mr. Haecker, T. Wallace Whittaker), are ultimately satirized because "there is no use toying with the reasons for living or dying, because whether one lives or kills himself is not really decided by philosophical reasons but by how one feels, and feelings are basically nonrational. " The objections of Hyman, Schickel, and Noland notwithstanding, the book's affirmative ending is "consistent and justified. "

C50 Tanner, Tony. "The Hoax That Joke Bilked, " Partisan Review, 34, 1 (1967), 102-09.

Barth's fiction centers around Wittgenstein's proposition that "the world is all that is the case. " His protagonists are so aware of the mind's ability to fabricate fictional alternatives that they can deny "any permanent value and stable meaning to the actual given world. " Personal identity particularly is viewed as a series of roles. Life is never more than a "motley confusion" for Todd Andrews; he merely resigns himself quixotically to participation. In The End of the Road, "both the narrator and his author appear to have what may be called a nominal sense of reality. " In effect, "the dialectic between life and mind has broken down and the dissociated consciousness drifts along in sterile isolation, sealed off in its own circular musings. " Barth's early work is characterized by this "absence of environment, " whereby he expresses the radical freedom of mind which, in American literature, is often posited as the alternative to radical subordination. In The Sot-Weed Factor, we read through the surface historical material to the book's two prevailing elements --"the formidable mental scope and [the] verbal dexterity of John Barth"--and thus witness "the dominance of words over things, the potent independence of sheer language. " In Giles Goat-Boy, Barth allows his computer-like intelligence to permutate categorical thinking until such a pitch of complexity is attained that discrimination must be abandoned entirely. One must accept that "the world simply is all that is the case, and that all things are of equal value, or nonvalue. Indeed they simply are. " Love may offer a means to that acceptance, or Barth may simply be saying that one can best survive by making sport of the conceptual possibilities which inundate us. In either case, mental gamesmanship in Giles Goat-Boy is carried beyond the point at which it became pernicious to the vitality of the novel.

C51 Tatham, Campbell. "The Gilesian Monomyth: Some Remarks on the Structure of Giles Goat-Boy, " Genre, 3, 4 (1970), 364-75.

Giles Goat-Boy "is far more indebted structurally to Campbell than to Raglan. " Point by point comparison between the systems of these two theorists and Barth's novel reveals

that he follows both scrupulously, but Campbell's program is
the more comprehensive and detailed of the two. Barth de-
parts from Campbell, however, on the issue of the final im-
port or purpose of the heroic quest. George's ultimate discovery is not Campbell's "all generating void" but "Ultimate
Paradox." He cannot communicate a universal doctrine--
"speak the unspeakable"--but only "speak about speaking the
unspeakable." One is left not with revelation, but with art.
"The boon which Giles and his creator offer to mankind is
not doctrine but artifact, the novel itself. Our delight must
be in the appreciation of the manipulation of aesthetic ulti-
macy, not in the discovery of Answers."

C52   . "John Barth and the Aesthetics of Artifice."
     Contemporary Literature, 12, 1 (1971), 60-73.

        Unlike many of his contemporaries, Barth "resolute-
ly denies the primacy of engagement with the moral imperative." His concern with external reality is exceptionally ten-
uous and specialized. "Barth's novels are commentaries on
theories of the novel; insofar as novels are a part of life,
Barth's novels are a commentary on a part of life." The
Floating Opera "is fundamentally concerned with the definition of the point of view involved in the act of artistic creation." The very existence of the novel Todd writes, and his
act of writing it, refute his contention that the universe is
completely irrational. "In other words, the nihilistic position
contains a contradiction, for the ability to perceive disorder
implies an ordered viewpoint; if nothing were ordered, the
novelist would be logically incapable of recognizing his own
position. Thus, Todd's clear and impressive ability to ma-
nipulate point of view demonstrates in itself a realm in which
order and meaning are apparently inherent. By insisting on
aesthetic artifice, he is able to construct a bulwark against
the acceptance of personal and universal irrationality; art
posits meaning, a momentary stay against encroaching confusion." In The Sot-Weed Factor Barth extends a concept of
the "presence" of the past employed by Borges and Eliot.
The contemporaneity of the themes, our awareness of the difference between the past and Barth's use of it, and his complex manipulation of plot and language again demonstrate that
art can be an ordering experience. The roman à clef element of Giles Goat-Boy is so contrived that "it would be absurd to take the allegorical level seriously." In a letter,
Barth states that these aspects " 'are deliberately laid on in
an obvious way, since they're the least central elements of
the fiction--a mere way of speaking.' " Giles ultimately dis-

covers "that there is no externally verifiable reality, that what is true depends utterly on one's point of view." He finds not meaning but "a way of talking about the impossibility of fixing meaning." Barth's aesthetic goal in all these enterprises is to produce "artifices which illuminate the process of thought rather than its end-product."

C53 Tilton, John W. "Giles Goat-Boy: An Interpretation," Bucknell Review, 28, 1 (1970), 92-119.

In Giles Goat-Boy Barth makes a comprehensive statement about the condition of man through the coordination of three myths: the Hero Myth, the Founder's Hill Myth, and the Boundary Dispute Myth. In the first, Giles, as representative of evolving human consciousness, transforms the original misanthropy of his mentor Max into self-sacrificial and life affirming love, routs the "dragon figure" Bray, who is the "personification of institutionalized religion," goes through a three-step enlightenment which culminates in his union with the Earth Goddess (Anastasia) and his Oriental-like realization of the unity of polarities. He leaves behind only the story of his life, The Revised New Syllabus, the record of his personal attainment of a truth that cannot be taught. In the second, Stoker's Powerhouse, located at the axis mundi, represents the "world navel," source of all creative energy. Stoker himself personifies the elemental dark power, innate in man and the universe, which must be balanced against the reason and light embodied in his brother Lucius Rexford--"two poles of the psyche which are integral components of the whole man." In the third, another internal rivalry between "two dimensions of the mind," selflessness and selfishness, is projected outward into the competition between East and West. Finally, "J.B.'s" unwillingness to accept the Posttape as authentic illustrates the inherent weakness which "almost guarantees that man will never harmonize the polarities of his psyche, never integrate the Evil One, never know himself as a whole embracing good and evil."

C54 Trachtenberg, Alan. "Barth and Hawkes: Two Fabulists," Critique, 6, 2 (1963), 4-18.

"Nothing is further from the truth than the idea some people have that Barth is a critic of modern manners." In fact, "Barth is a fabulist, mainly concerned with man's mind, not his society." He focuses on "the problem of existence and identity," particularly as manifest in the disease of

"cosmopsis." The issue carries through all three novels.
Captain Adam "will become ... a mysterious Doctor and an
incredible Burlingame. And Todd, whose suicide fails, will
become Jake Horner." Todd, Jake, and Eben, in their unwillingness to judge and their need for identity, resemble
Huck Finn; Burlingame, in his flights of fancy and manipulation of appearances, resembles Tom Sawyer. "Burlingame
and the Doctor are versions of an American Dream, of freedom from responsibility, from the pains and perils of selfhood." Like Hawkes, Barth implies that traditional novelistic
realism is depleted. "Barth's fables are based on intellectual attitudes embodied in character and action. But his stories
are not allegories; they are sufficiently 'realistic' for us to
recognize common human behavior.... He creates the appear-
ance, through great erudition, of a highly artificial surface,
in order to show how arbitrary, how un-necessary, are all
human conventions. One gets the feeling throughout The Sot-
Weed Factor that Barth is parodying his own form."

BOOKS

D1 Bryant, Jerry H. The Open Decision: The Contempo-
    rary American Novel and Its Intellectual Background.
    New York: Free Press, 1970.

D2 Godshalk, William L. "Cabell and Barth: Our Comic
    Athletes," in Louis D. Rubin, Jr., ed. The Comic
    Imagination in American Literature (New Brunswick,
    N.J.: Rutgers University Press, 1973), pp. 275-83.

        This short study argues that Cabell's "resolute fri-
volity" and Barth's "cheerful nihilism" is, for each of them,
"a way of dealing with pessimism." The similarity of attitude (Barth's being the darker of the two) leads to similarities of artistic procedure. Cabell and Barth both engage in
serious literary gamesmanship, ironically employing history
and myth to demonstrate the world's lack of inherent meaning
and value.

D3 Harris, Charles B. Contemporary American Novelists
    of the Absurd. New Haven, Conn.: College and
    University Press, 1971. [See item E19.]

D4 Hauck, Richard Boyd. "These Fruitful Odysseys: John
    Barth," in his A Cheerful Nihilism: Confidence and
    "the Absurd" in American Humorous Fiction (Bloom-
    ington: Indiana University Press, 1971), pp. 201-36.

        In a largely synoptic survey of Barth's work from
The Floating Opera to Giles Goat-Boy, Hauck argues that
Barth's reliance upon artifice and humor stems directly from
his recognition of the Absurd: "What is hilarious is the way
men accept models of reality as reality and forget that the
model has a story reality of its own."

D5 Joseph, Gerhard. John Barth. Minneapolis: Univer-
    sity of Minnesota Press, 1970. (University of Minne-
    sota Pamphlets on American Writers, no. 91.)

In this perceptive "interim account of Barth's development" up to and including Lost in the Funhouse, Joseph contends that, although the novels are not academic in the conventional sense, "the educational experience either as theme or all-encompassing metaphor is central to each of them." Barth's technique has progressively altered from time-bound "regional verisimilitude" to the timeless "mythic configurations" of fable.

D6   Klinkowitz, Jerome. "Preface" and "Prologue: The Death of the Death of the Novel," in his Literary Disruptions: The Making of a Post-Contemporary American Fiction (Urbana: University of Illinois Press, 1975), pp. ix-x and 1-32.

Klinkowitz argues that a new term and a new understanding must be developed to facilitate the acceptance of those writers who are in fact superseding the standard "contemporary" writers. "My thesis is that the most contemporary of this lot, Barth and Pynchon, are in fact regressive parodists, who by the Literature of Exhaustion theory have confused the course of American fiction and held back the critical (although not popular) appreciation of Kurt Vonnegut, Jr., Donald Barthelme, Jerzy Kosinski and the other writers [including Imamu Baraka, James Park Sloan, Ronald Sukenick, Raymond Federman, and Gilbert Sorrentino] surveyed in this book." Barth and Pynchon indulge in "polite thematic (and not formal) revolt from what has gone before" and are therefore "funereal" in their effect upon fiction. Barth's essay, "The Literature of Exhaustion" must be read as either "a literary suicide note" or "an equivocation." Lost in the Funhouse does not effectively substantiate Barth's declared aesthetic. Chimera is "an allegory of his own exhaustions" which "confuses the product of art with the conditions of its inception"--a process that "often results in simple bad writing." Finally, "it is precisely because Barth has suffered an exhaustion (if not castration) of the imagination that his fiction falters."

D7   Kostelanetz, Richard. "The New American Fiction," in his The New American Arts (New York: Horizon Press, 1965), pp. 194-236; especially pp. 203-12.

In a general defense of the continuing vitality of American fiction, John Barth is characterized as "unquestionably the most brilliant and promising novelist to appear in America in the past ten years." He is praised for his in-

telligence, erudition, and inventiveness. His career is said
to evidence such a steadily increasing maturity that "the potential limits of Barth's achievements are beyond pre-defini-
tion, if not comprehension." The Sot-Weed Factor is "a
mockery of written history" in which Barth systematical-
ly distorts and debunks accepted notions of the past. At
the same time, it parodies an array of literary conventions and invests its satire with universal significance. The
Floating Opera, however, "is stylistically undistinguished and,
once the joke is fathomed, not very interesting." The End of
the Road is weaker still--"uneven in tone, uninteresting in
language, never quite focusing on the announced theme--
Horner's evasion of responsibility--and lacking any other unifying thread." Giles Goat-Boy promises to be even more extraordinary than The Sot-Weed Factor. Barth seems to be
engaged in a progressively more inclusive elaboration of his
essential theme. "The world yields to our efforts no ordering scheme; there is no central truth, only nonsense, with
each twist of complexity multiplying itself to infinite degrees."

D8   Lebowitz, Naomi. Humanism and the Absurd in the
        Modern Novel (Evanston, Ill.: Northwestern Univer-
        sity Press, 1971), pp. 123-26.

        In a section distinguishing between humanist and ab-
surdist parody, Barth is cited as a prime example of the latter. He is said to manifest an astounding capacity to manip-
ulate literary materials, but this "decontamination from the
world" forces his imagination to feed only upon itself. "Each
novelty, released from the bounds of mere experience, can
take us in but once; the absurdist's wit is tarnished by self-
plagiarism. He uses parody to spring himself from moral
and aesthetic commitments or expectations, while the human-
ist uses parody in the same way that he uses history--in the
service, not the mastery, of contemporary life." Such
writers practice self-preservation through evasion. "The absurdist will not let his characters get their hooks into him,
nor will he give them the opportunity to diminish him. He
saves his identity by outwitting them." Thus in novels like
The Sot-Weed Factor "history and literature and their pre-
tenses of truth are teased, but the process of transvaluation
never translates the epistemological problem into a moral
one."

D9   Olderman, Raymond M. Beyond the Waste Land: A
        Study of the American Novel in the Nineteen Sixties.
        New York: Free Press, 1970. [See item E32.]

D10   Scholes, Robert. "Fabulation and Epic Vision," in his
        The Fabulators (New York: Oxford University Press,
        1967), pp. 135-173.

        In this apology for fabulation as a distinct and legiti-
mate response to the dissipation of realism, Giles Goat-Boy
is described as "an epic to end all epics, and a sacred book
to end all sacred books" which manifests all the essential
characteristics of the mode--delight in design, primacy of
language over its referents, ideationally determined structure.
The work is analyzed primarily in terms of its linguistic fu-
sions; its two fundamental metaphors (the universe as university and the hero as goat); and its historical-sociological,
fictional-mythic, and philosophical-allegorical dimensions,
each of which grows naturally out of the other. "For every
thoughtful person, the world is a university, and his education always in process." George's archetypal quest through
Thesis and Antithesis leads to a Synthesis that entails personal action and personal responsibility in a world devoid of all
external guides. "Passage and failure are distinct but inter-
dependent. They define one another and are as necessary as
North and South or male and female to the functioning of the
universe. Action by each individual, appropriate to himself
and his situation, discovered by the dialectic process of trial
and error, is the only way to salvation. Thus there are no
formulas."

D11   Schulz, Dieter. "John Barth," in Martin Christalder,
          ed., Amerikanische Literatur der Gegenwart (Stutt-
          gart: Alfred Kroner, 1973), pp. 371-90.

D12   Stark, John O. The Literature of Exhaustion: Borges,
          Nabokov, and Barth. Durham, N.C.: Duke Univer-
          sity Press, 1974.

        A general discussion of these three writers in regard
to the idea of Exhaustion as discussed in Barth's essay, and
individual chapters on the particular irrealistic techniques of
each.

D13   Tanner, Tony. "What Is the Case?," in his City of
          Words: American Fiction, 1950-1970 (New York:
          Harper and Row, 1971), pp. 230-59.

        Incorporating his previously published observations,
Tanner argues that Barth's art exploits the tension between
what is the case (if, indeed, such can even be determined)

and arbitrary, often playful, verbal construct. Barth begins
with "a sense that verbal play precedes existence and experience," which leads him, like many contemporary American
writers, into an ambiance of "ambiguous freedom." Survey-
ing the novels in order, Tanner detects a growing insistence
upon personal control which leads ultimately, in Lost in the
Funhouse, to a potentially pernicious lack of connectedness
with external experience.

D14   Tharpe, Jac.   John Barth: The Comic Sublimity of
        Paradox.   Carbondale: Southern Illinois University
        Press, 1974.

    The first full-length critical book devoted exclusively
to John Barth.   The work attempts to survey the whole terri-
tory from The Floating Opera to Chimera, including Barth's
metaphysics, ethics, epistemology, character types, themes,
narrative techniques, and career phases.   It does so with
great verve and with many sporadic insights, but without unifying focus.   The result is a rich and provocative catalogue,
repeatedly illustrating the paradoxical nature of Barth's art,
but substantiating no particular thesis.

DISSERTATIONS*

E1   Allen, Mary Inez. "The Necessary Blankness: Women in Major American Fiction of the Sixties," University of Maryland, 1973. (DAI, 34, 12, 7736-A.)

Barth is among eight novelists whose work is surveyed in this study. These writers "do not differ significantly in seeing women as bleak characters who become hysterical in their lack of activity and control over their lives." The males, however, are more inclined to portray the bitch mother, to view power as residing in women, and to imply distance between themselves and their female characters.

E2   Bailey, Dennis Lee. "The Modern Novel in the Presence of Myth," Purdue University, 1974. (DAI, 35, 11, 7292-A.)

This dissertation offers a theoretical approach labeled "structural hermeneutic" which "develops Levi-Strauss' concept of binary opposition as an analytic strategy to include the opposition between the individual and his community." Myth mediates between these poles. Giles Goat-Boy utilizes narrative self-consciousness, the metaphor of the university, and a protagonist who has "the dual tasks of mediating between elaborate sets of binary characters and of discovering his own role within the community."

E3   Bazzanella, Dominic John. "The Mad Narrator in Contemporary Fiction," Northwestern University, 1970. (DAI, 31, 10, 5387-A.)

---

*For each dissertation, the location is given of its entry in Dissertation Abstracts International [i.e., DAI]: Abstracts of Dissertations Available on Microfilm or As Xerographic Reproductions (Ann Arbor, Mich.: Xerox University Microfilms, 1938- ; title has varied). Masters' theses are not included in this portion of the bibliography.

The Floating Opera and The End of the Road are
among other contemporary works analyzed to determine the
role of the mad narrator. Such a narrator is simultaneously aware of two worlds, one inner, one outer, which he attempts to reconcile. He fails, however, because his inner
world is always more significant to him than reality, sometimes to such a degree that it utterly displaces reality. The
author who creates this persona must be carefully distinguished from his creation. "He self-consciously stands apart
from his mad narrator by undermining the narrator's credibility and his narrative authenticity." Narrative of this sort
demands a sophisticated and creative readership. "The
reader who discovers the authorial consciousness that lies
above the mad narrative consciousness discovers the realm
of the creative imagination which enables the artist to transcend the obsessively limited imagination of the madman."
Reading such works is thus an exercise in differentiating between positive imaginativeness and madness. The writers
who create them "remain at least implicitly optimistic and
celebrate the possibility, if not the probability of human
achievement."

E4   Begnal, Mary Kate. "Self-Mimesis in the Fiction of
      John Barth," Pennsylvania State University, 1974.
      (DAI, 35, 11, 7293-A.)

        "A case is made for the judgment that Barth's work
tends from his earliest novels toward self-mimesis, toward
an imitation of the artistic process and the artistic self that
finally seeks to break out into some radical contact with life
and its root problems." Through parody of form (studied
with reference to particular models for each novel) Barth
seeks to jettison moribund structures in order to confront
experience afresh. In his later fiction, Barth makes heavy
use of the artist figure as a creative link between man and
absolutes, and man and man. Such fusion is achieved through
"a synthesis of art and love."

E5   Bienstock, Beverly Gray. "The Self-Conscious Artist
      in Contemporary American Fiction," University of
      California, Los Angeles, 1973. (DAI, 34, 11, 7219-
      A.)

        One of the dissertation's four chapters is devoted to
John Barth. "Close study indicates that Barth's novels are
all concerned with the role of the artist." From Giles Goat-
Boy on, he begins to "include himself in his works." Lost

in the Funhouse deals with the author as Narcissus and Echo,
particularly in light of McLuhan's predictions. Chimera ex-
amines "the crucial relationship between teller, tale, and
told." In all these works, "Barth simultaneously questions
the power of the artist and reveals his own commitment to
art."

E6   Billings, Philip Allan. "John Barth's Initial Trilogy:
      A Study of the Themes of Value and Identity in The
      Floating Opera, The End of the Road, and The Sot-
      Weed Factor," Michigan State University, 1974.
      (DAI, 35, 9, 6129-A.)

      Taken together, these three novels "make a coher-
ent and complete statement on the possibility of modern man's
achieving a sense of value and identity in the nihilistic universe." There is a progress from the elimination of abso-
lutist possibilities, to the elimination of rationalist ethics,
to an intuitive "paradoxical synthesis of recognition of the
loss of absolutes and insistence on their necessity, a combination of experience and innocence." Thus a " 'Higher Innocence' " is attained when one acts as if identity and value exist. This state is symbolized in the successful, though il-
lusion-free, marital relationship.

E7   Bufithis, Philip Henry. "The Artist's Fight for Art:
      The Psychiatrist Figure in the Fiction of Major Con-
      temporary American Novelists," University of Penn-
      sylvania, 1971. (DAI, 32, 4, 2083-A.)

      "Through its examination of eight American novelists
this study reveals two basic attitudes--so basic as to be almost axioms: (1) The fiction of major contemporary American novelists has conceived of the psychiatrist figure as a
character against whom the artist-protagonist defines himself.
(2) These novelists propound a faith in art and the creation
of art as primal values."

E8   Cantrill, Dante Kenneth. "Told by an Idiot: Toward
      an Understanding of Modern Fiction Through an An-
      alysis of the Works of William Faulkner and John
      Barth," University of Washington, 1974. (DAI, 35,
      7, 4505-A.)

      Modern relativism has fostered a new view of the
relationship between actuality and imagination: "reality, once
thought to yield only to imitation in art, is actually only a

framework of the individual imagination; every person is a poet, a fiction-maker, to the extent that he is imaginative, and the appropriate symbol is no longer Daedalus but Arachne, weaving from her bowels a life-sustaining fabrication." Faulkner and Barth are treated in such a way as to demonstrate that each promotes this attitude and that the fiction of each "can be interpreted in terms of the relationship between the concepts of reality and fiction and between fiction and fiction-maker."

E9   Ciancio, Ralph Armando. "The Grotesque in Modern American Fiction: An Existential Theory," University of Pittsburgh, 1964. (DAI, 26, 1, 365-A.)

The works of John Barth and others supply practical examples to support a theory on the nature, causes, and aims of the grotesque.

E10   Clauss, Anne R. "Digression as Narrative Technique in Contemporary Fiction," University of Wisconsin, 1970. (DAI, 31, 9, 4758-A.)

Barth is one of four contemporary novelists whose works are examined in relation to the long tradition of digressive narration. All of Barth's pre-1970 novels are considered because they represent "a wide range of possibility" for a technique particularly well suited to the contemporary writer because it offers "a means of capturing a hostile and fugitive reality."

E11   Decker, Sharon Davie. "Passionate Virtuosity: The Fiction of John Barth," University of Virginia, 1972. (DAI, 33, 7, 3639-A.)

Barth is primarily concerned with the problem of meaning--the world's apparent lack of it, and how one goes about creating it in experience. "Both the form and content of his fiction explore two avenues of escape from meaninglessness: creative energy; and love, involvement with others." The search for a "passionate virtuosity" leads to two related issues: "the ambivalence of language as a tool for ordering experience, the corrupt or creative role it can play; and in the later fiction, the ambivalent nature of reality itself, whether it is governed ultimately by multiplicity or an encircling unity."

E12   Elgin, Donald Deane. "The Rogue Appears: A Study

of the Development of the Picaresque in Modern
American Fiction, " Vanderbilt University, 1973.
(DAI, 34, 7, 4256-A.)

One chapter is given to detailed analysis of the Sot-
Weed Factor. "This work is seen as demonstrating a modification in the traditional picaresque point of view and as add-
ing a mask tradition and a greater capacity for abstraction to the traditional capabilities of the picaro."

E13   Fogel, Stanley Howard. "Ludic Fiction--Metafiction:
       The Contemporary Experimental Novel in America, "
       Purdue University, 1973. (DAI, 35, 1, 447-A.)

Barth is one of five novelists interpreted as ludic
artists. Such an artist is "imbued with the awareness that
societal and artistic constructs are game-spheres with arbitrary rules." This awareness "impels him to create unique
constructs within which he often explores and parodies exist-
ing structures and their laws."

E14   Fort, Deborah Charnley. "Contrast Epic: A Study of
       Joseph Heller's Catch 22 (1961), Gunter Grass's The
       Tin Drum (Die Blechtrommel [1959]), John Barth's
       The Sot-Weed Factor (1960, Revised 1967), and Vlad-
       imir Nabokov's Pale Fire (1962), " University of
       Maryland, 1974. (DAI, 35, 6, 3677-A.)

The term "contrast epic" is adapted from Frye and
refers to works which "use epic tradition as contrast against
the contemporary reality their protagonists face." In mock
epic, "the sordid present is treated ironically in relation to
a glorious past, " but contrast epic reverses this relationship
by demonstrating the ludicrousness of adherence to heroic tradition in an unheroic world. The particular points of reference for The Sot-Weed Factor are the Iliad, the Odyssey,
the Aeneid, Hudibras, and Tom Jones.

E15   Gildsdorf, Jeanette Wortman. "The Multiple Perspec-
       tive in Modern Experimental Novels: Eight Examples, "
       University of Nebraska--Lincoln, 1974. (DAI, 36, 2,
       878-A.)

"The multiple-narrator trick in Giles Goat-Boy ...
consists of a series of concentric frame devices enclosing the
main tale, itself told on no certain authority.... Numerous
short pieces in Lost in the Funhouse..., each with a different

kind of narrative voice, all concern a universal artist represented by Ambrose M--. "

E16 Golden, Daniel. "Shapes and Strategies: Forms of
Modern American Fiction in the Novels of Robert
Penn Warren, Saul Bellow, and John Barth," Indiana
University, 1972. (DAI, 33, 6, 2933-A.)

Barth's early works are "novels of ideas or philosophical novels, depicting existential men of atrophied sensibilities, unable to impose significant order on their world. "
In his later work, Barth creates "the anti-historical novel,
the anti-Bildungsroman, and numerous other parodic genres. "
Through this enterprise, in combination with his mockery of
the artist role itself, Barth implies that "the techniques as
well as the subjects of narrative art have been exhausted. "

E17 Gourevitch, Mary Turzills. "The Writer as Double
Agent: Essay on the Conspiratorial Mode in Contemporary Fiction," Case Western Reserve University, 1970. (DAI, 31, 7, 3547-A.)

"The impossibility of finding suitable comforting lies
to cover up what is most appalling in man's condition is demonstrated in John Barth's novel, The End of the Road. In
this novel, popularized existential ideas are evaluated as a
means of dealing with the human condition, and these ideas
are discredited through parody. "

E18 Gresham, James Thomas. "John Barth as Menippean
Satirist," Michigan State University, 1972. (DAI,
33, 9, 5176-A.)

A definition of Menippean satire (including a lengthy
catalogue of its specific attributes) is developed with particular reference to the observations of Northrop Frye. Its use
is surveyed in the works of Petronius, Lucian, Cervantes,
Swift, Voltaire, Sterne, Burton, Joyce, Rabelais, and others.
The most essential difference between conventional and Menippean satire is found to be that its norm "is not the Good
or the Ideal, but the Real. " It has, therefore, a different
end. "Lucidity--perception of 'reality'--is the goal, and the
delusory ideal is generally viewed as a manifestation of Romance or rubricizing. "

E19 Harris, Charles B. "Contemporary American Novelists of the Absurd, " Southern Illinois University,

1970. (DAI, 31, 8, 4162-A.)

Barth is one of four novelists whose work is studied as a fusion between absurdist vision and absurdist technique.

E20 Intrater, Roseline. "The Attrition of Self in Some Contemporary Novels," Case Western Reserve University, 1970. (DAI, 31, 7, 3550-A.)

Barth is one of three Anglo-American writers whose work is studied in light of the attrition of self induced by Absurdity, Nothingness, Fragmentation, and Externality. These writers are so heavily influenced by Sartre and Camus that their productions "may be read as commentaries upon the theories advanced by these writers."

E21 Janoff, Bruce Lee. "Beyond Satire: Black Humor in the Novels of John Barth and Joseph Heller," Ohio University, 1972. (DAI, 33, 4, 1728-A.)

The Floating Opera and The End of the Road are interpreted as representing, respectively, the comic and despairing poles of black humor, a phenomenon distinguished from traditional satire by virtue of being more metaphysical than sociological, more rebellious than didactic, and "aimed not so much at the affirmation of art and life as at the negation of silence and lifelessness."

E22 Johnstone, Douglas Blake. "Myth and Psychology in the Novels of John Barth," University of Oregon, 1973. (DAI, 34, 9, 5973-A.)

Mythology and psychology merge in the "deep structure" of Barth's works. In each novel the protagonist is a "prodigal Oedipus" who is separated (often through no fault of his own) from his father and who, plagued by guilt, feels a need to reunite and win forgiveness. This guilt of separation arises from a subconscious craving for the mother, a craving which renders all other male-female relationships untenable. Eventually, the protagonist is denied psychological maturity when he relinquishes sexuality and reattaches himself to the father.

E23 Jordan, Enock Pope, III. "A Critical Study of the Textual Variants in John Barth's Novels: The Floating Opera, The End of the Road, and The Sot-Weed Factor," University of Oklahoma, 1974. (DAI, 35, 4, 2273-A.)

"The revisions in all three novels demonstrate Barth's maturation as a fictional stylist; they reveal a craftsman with a greater sensitivity to the sound and structure of prose, a more comprehensive grasp of the effects produced by the narrative voice, and a clearer awareness of narrative pace." Such changes make greater demands for the reader's participation and suggest that "Barth's fictions are shaped to a considerable extent by his conception of his reading audience."

E24 Josenhans, Elinor Louise. "Form in the Fiction of John Barth," Fordham University, 1974. (DAI, 35, 5, 2993-A.)

"Barth contends that language is the matter of his books and each book results from a particular language pattern. He considers himself an orchestrator of the old literary devices. Such an approach is designed pointedly to make the reader conscious of form." The development of this aesthetic is traced by devoting one chapter to each work from The Floating Opera to Lost in the Funhouse.

E25 Kennard, Jean Elizabeth. "Towards a Novel of the Absurd: A Study of the Relationship Between the Concept of the Absurd as Defined in the Works of Sartre and Camus and Ideas of Form in the Fiction of John Barth, Samuel Beckett, Nigel Dennis, Joseph Heller, and James Purdy," University of California, Berkeley. 1968. (DAI, 29, 9, 3144-A.)

By employing a number of anti-rational techniques-- "impossible events without causal connection, circular structure, characters who change identity, logic which destroys sense, language which illustrates the inadequacies of language"--the novel of the absurd brings about the experience of the absurd (as described by Sartre and Camus) in its reader. One is induced, that is, to demand meaning where none is available. Such a novel thus becomes "a metaphor for itself."

E26 Klein, James Robert. "The Tower and the Maze: A Study of the Novels of John Barth," University of Illinois at Urbana-Champaign, 1971. (DAI, 32, 10, 5794-A.)

The metaphors of the tower and the maze are drawn from "Lost in the Funhouse." the labyrinth motif, "Barth's image of contemporary consciousness and of our world," has

its nucleus in The Floating Opera, takes on social implications in The End of the Road, encompasses history and myth
in The Sot-Weed Factor, and comes to represent "nearly all
of man's collective creation" in Giles Goat-Boy. "All of
Barth's protagonists are lost in funhouse worlds they are incapable of organizing into heroic plots, and each, like Ambrose, comes to terms with his world and himself by writing
ironic, self-conscious funhouse narration about his failed in-
tercourse with the world." These productions resemble satire, except that they are "both ethically and aesthetically less
certain" than their 18th-century predecessors. Thus they
emphasize "diffractions and distortions" rather than clear
morality and wit, and utilize deliberate narrative confusion
rather than the precision of the heroic couplet. Barth uses
the tower image to represent that part of himself and his
protagonists which tends to use the novel as a means of at-
taining dominance of perspective and personal dimension.
Hence, in each work there is a struggle between the anti-
novel and the novel.

E27   Laughman, Celeste Marie.   "Mirrors and Masks in the
      Novels of John Barth," University of Massachusetts,
      1971. (DAI, 32, 3, 1519-A.)

      "In the familiar contemporary atmosphere of flux and
uncertainty which is the world of the novels, man's attempts
to live coherently, to impose order and values on his life are
seen as masks, human constructs which, while often inhibit-
ing direct response to feeling, disguise and protect man from
the mutability and disorder which lie beneath them. Mirrors
penetrate the masks by revealing hidden or submerged truths,
at times salutary as well as destructive, about the character
and nature of our lives."

E28   LeClair, Thomas Edmund.   "Final Words: Death and
      Comedy in the Fiction of Donleavy, Hawkes, Barth
      Vonnegut, and Percy," Duke University, 1972. (DAI,
      33, 10, 5731-A.)

      "Barth's fiction, especially his first two novels The
Floating Opera and The End of the Road, reveals characters
who flee the threat of death by adopting aesthetic models for
the self."

E29   McClintick, Michael Lloyd.   "The Comic Hero: A Study
      of the Mythopoeic Imagination in the Novel," Wash-
      ington State University, 1974. (DAI, 35, 1, 409-A.)

Frye's aesthetics and Jung's psychology are here
united to derive a concept of the comic hero that stresses
the reader's perception of the protagonist's relationship to
the world, rather than traditional notions of comedy and heroism. "The comic hero, facing an unsympathetic society,
imaginatively remolds that society in terms of his own vision." Ebenezer Cooke is one example of the Don Quixote
prototype.

E30 Miller, Norman. "The Self-Conscious Narrator-Pro-
tagonist in American Fiction Since World War II,"
University of Wisconsin, 1972. (DAI, 32, 10, 5798-
A.)

The Floating Opera is one of ten novels surveyed.
As a type, the self-conscious narrator-protagonist is an alienated individual who seeks to justify himself through the
writing experience. He is, therefore, somewhat unreliable,
and the reader "must perceive the irony that develops between
the story he tells and the 'story' of his attempt to shape it
to his own ends in order to determine the author's perspective."

E31 Morrell, David Bernard. "John Barth: An Introduc-
tion," Pennsylvania State University, 1970. (DAI,
31, 9, 4784-A.)

The dissertation makes use of manuscripts, unpub-
lished essays and letters, and interviews with Barth, his
agent, and his editors. One basic situation is found to per-
vade all of Barth's first five books. His characters, all
temperamentally compelled to analyze a condition they consider intolerable, arrive ultimately at two fundamental givens:
"one, that life always gets worse, never simpler, never eas-
ier, never meaningfuller; two, that things are what they are
rather than something else." In despair, these characters
then indulge in role playing and the fabrication of alternative
worlds, until reality again intrudes to such a degree that they
must either change roles or else face the options of suicide,
paralysis, or silence.

E32 Olderman, Raymond Michael. "Beyond the Waste Land:
A Study of the American Novel in the Nineteen-Six-
ties," Indiana University, 1969. (DAI, 30, 11, 4998-
A.)

Barth is considered among the authors of 13 novels

representative of the major drift of the American novel in the Sixties. The tradition of romance is continued, with a move in the direction of fable. A characteristic vision develops, involving "a sense that fact and fiction have become completely indistinguishable; a fear of some force--an institution or a. malicious conspiracy--that has seized control over the life of the individual; and the driving need to affirm life over death no matter how radical an act is required for that affirmation." Finally, the image of the waste land "has replaced the 'American Dream' as the controlling metaphor for American romance. "

E33   Plater, William Marmaduke. "Metaphormosis: An Examination of Communication and Community in Barth, Beckett and Pynchon," University of Illinois at Urbana-Champaign, 1973. (DAI, 34, 12, 7776-A.)

Barth, Beckett and Pynchon, all engage in turning experience into speech and, self-consciously aware of the falsifications this necessitates, create a kind of art that reveals the true nature of language. "The tension ... is always between community and individuality, between language--the basis of community--and experience--a unique and private consciousness prior to language." Lost in the Funhouse is the Barth book used to illustrate the general pattern of a protagonist who begins by searching for meaning, becomes aware of the inadequacy of language, grows alienated to the point of considering himself mentally ill, and finally reintegrates himself by affirming the metaphoric nature of language and resolving to live in society as an "adroit falsifier."

E34   Reilly, Charles Edward. "The Ancient Roots of Modern Satiric Fiction: An Analysis of 'Petronian' and 'Apuleian' Elements in the Novels of John Barth, J. P. Donleavy, Joseph Heller, James Joyce, and Vladimir Nabokov," University of Delaware, 1974. (DAI, 35, 4, 2293-A.)

Pale Fire and Chimera fit the definition of Apuleian satiric fiction because they focus on the problem of finding peace and meaning in an absurd and amoral world, champion the idea that these qualities can only be attained by "rejecting worldly allurements and pursuing ideal truths," and use allegorical representations of "the human mind as it rises above the agonies of everyday existence through the godlike act of literary creation. "

E35   St. Germain, Amos Joseph. "Religious Interpretation
      and Contemporary Literature: Kurt Vonnegut, Jr.,
      Robert Coover and John Barth," University of Iowa,
      1974. (DAI, 35, 7, 4552-A.)

      In these authors one finds "little concern with formal
theology but a marked concern with social morality." Barth
relentlessly pursues the implications of existentialism and
pragmatism. "By his use of religious traditions and structures, Barth maintains that philosophical and theological spec-
ulations, as well as other intellectual and artistic activity,
are useless." He maintains that literature is responsible only to itself and subjects all his provisional solutions to prag-
matic testing.

E36   Scofield, James Davis. "Absurd Man and the Esthetics
      of the Absurd: The Fiction of John Barth," Kent
      State University, 1973. (DAI, 34, 7, 4285-A.)

      "John Barth's work presents a view of man and fic-
tion itself as absurd.... The problem of living in a relativ-
istic world faced by Barth's early heroes becomes in his
later work the esthetic dilemma of stories with nothing to as-
sert and which must portray an artistic doubt and indecision
.... Thus, Barth seems to choose an art whose expression
is that there is nothing to express, perhaps even little desire
for expressing this nothing, and a recognition of the arbitrariness of bothering with writing under these conditions. Yet
the paradox is that the writer is left with the compulsion to
express something, even if only this very predicament."

E37   Shapiro, Stephen Alan. "The Ambivalent Animal: Man
      in the Contemporary British and American Novel,"
      University of Washington, 1965. (DAI, 26, 5, 2760-
      A.)

      The End of the Road is one of many contemporary
novels which "compel the reader to recognize the areas of
ambiguity in human affairs and require the critic to consider
the kind of creature who creates and responds to ambiguity in
actual life and in literary structures."

E38   Tatham, Campbell. "The Novels of John Barth: An In-
      troduction," University of Wisconsin, 1968. (DAI,
      29, 1, 4471-A.)

      Each of Barth's first four novels "assumes the basic

tenet of contemporary existentialism"--namely, that reality is "disordered, irrational, impenetrable, and contingent." Each protagonist, consequently, tends to "envision external chaos in terms of personal, internal fragmentation and basic animality." The tension between such flux and the desire for consistent individual being leads to various identity crises involving self-projection, masks, and doubles. Only fiction itself offers a workable and therapeutic alternative, for "within the actuality of the artifact, order and self-knowledge are possible." Although Barth persistently refuses to engage in ordinary social commentary, his fictions have the effect of causing the reader to reconsider the nature of fiction and its relationship to reality. "Life, Barth implies, becomes a question of point of view...."

E39   Tenenbaum, Elizabeth Brody.   "Concepts of the Self in
        the Modern Novel," Stanford University, 1972.   (DAI,
        32, 12, 7010-A.)

    In The End of the Road, Barth repudiates the basis for the psychological novel by suggesting that the private self is illusory. He is therefore akin to Ralph Ellison in Invisible Man. "The narrator-protagonists of these two novels cannot be defined by either their inherent characteristics or their freely chosen acts. The only coherence that either possesses is that of a unique consciousness structuring reality in its own way."

E40   Thomas, Jesse James.   "The Image of Man in the Lit-
        erary Heroes of Jean-Paul Sartre and Three Ameri-
        can Novelists: Saul Bellow, John Barth, and Ken
        Kesey--A Theological Evaluation," Northwestern Uni-
        versity, 1967.   (DAI, 28, 6, 233-A.)

    "John Barth's Ebenezer Cooke and George Giles arrive at an authentic realization that 'innocence' (detachment) is guilt and that life is suffering on behalf of others, yet the ultimate picture of the universe is still colored with more gloom than joy."

E41   Turner, Theodore Baker, III.   "Mind Forged Manacles:
        Images of the University in American Fiction of the
        Nineteen Sixties; A Study in Kesey, Mailer, Barth,
        Bellow, Nabokov, and Burroughs," University of Iowa,
        1974.   (DAI, 35, 7, 4566-A.)

    This study "looks at the specific fictional cases developed by each author, in which an individual molded by educational institutions and American society tries to assert his own will and forge his own life. These cases constitute serious challenges to the academy."

E42 Urbanski, Kenneth John. "The Forming Artifice in John Barth's Fictions," University of Kansas, 1973. (DAI, 34, 12, 7789-A.)

Barth is studied as the prime exemplar of a tendency in contemporary American fiction to oppose traditional realistic modes with works that reflect the compositional process itself. Traditional critical methods and vocabularies are found to be inadequate, and the term "forming artifice" is offered as a substitute for "the ambiguous concepts of form and content."

E43 Valencia, Willa Feree. "The Picaresque Tradition in the Contemporary English and American Novel," University of Illinois, 1968. (DAI, 29, 2, 618-A.)

The works of 12 American writers of "neo-picaresque" are found to be "less faithful to the historical picaresque tradition than their English counterparts, owing, in part, to the American predilection for romance as opposed to the novel of manners."

E44 Weixlmann, Joseph Norman, Jr. "Counter-Types and Anti-Myths: Black and Indian Characters in the Fiction of John Barth," Kansas State University, 1973. (DAI, 34, 6, 3439-A.)

In Barth's aesthetics, the manner in which characters function is more important than what they signify. Barth's most prevalent method for dealing with Black and Indian characters is "counter-typing," the use of "stereotypical figures who become forceful comedic characterizations via the hyperbole with which they are presented." One byproduct of this technique is the reduction of stereotyped notions to absurdity. A secondary method, "anti-mythologizing," consists of "comedic exposé of the underlying 'truth' which renders some of America's most sacred myths apocryphal." Perhaps the best example of this technique is Barth's handling of the Pocahontas-John Smith story. Many of the names in The Sot-Weed Factor are drawn from the glossary of Virginia Indian language in the second book of Smith's Generall Historie and from the Archives of Maryland.

E45 Wilson, George Robert. "The Quest Romance in Con-
          temporary Fiction," Florida State University, 1968.
          (DAI, 30, 2, 741-A.)

          Giles Goat-Boy is one contemporary example among
several of the difference between the romance and the novel
--a distinction developed from observations made by Northrop Frye and Richard Chase.